BRANCH LINES TO
NEWPORT

Vic Mitchell and Keith Smith

The Isle of Wight Steam Railway extended its operation to Smallbrook Junction on 21st July 1991 and reopened Ashey on 2nd May 1993.

Congratulations to all concerned with these achievements.

First published July 1985
Revised and reprinted September 1988
2nd reprint June 1994

ISBN 0 906520 26 6

Cover design Deborah Goodridge

Published by Middleton Press
          Easebourne Lane
          Midhurst
          West Sussex
          GU29 9AZ
          Tel: (0730) 813169
(From 16 April 1995 - (01730) 813169)

Printed & bound by Biddles Ltd,
          Guildford and Kings Lynn

CONTENTS

INDEX

ACKNOWLEDGEMENTS

Our grateful thanks go to all those mentioned in the captions not only for providing prints or loaning photographs but also for help with information in many cases. Thanks also go to A.A.F. Bell, N. Langridge for the loan of tickets; to H. Hunt for help with IWCR timetables; to R. Randall for research assistance; to Mrs. E. Fisk and N. Stanyon for proof reading and to our ever helpful wives.

GEOGRAPHICAL SETTING

The Cowes to Sandown line followed the broad, almost level, valley of the River Medina as far as Newport. At this place the valley cuts through the Central Chalk Ridge of the island and the line ran parallel to the now tiny River Medina as far as Blackwater, continuing close to one of its tributaries almost to Merstone Junction. Here the watershed was crossed, the railway then running down the shallow valley of the River Yar until turning sharply out of it, just before reaching Sandown. The Ventnor West branch from Merstone Junction climbed along the upper part of the valley of the small River Yar, passing its source close to the entrance to the tunnel. This tunnel pierced the chalk mass of the Southern Downs and brought the line out onto a shelf on the cliffs of the south coast, along which it continued to its terminus.

The Ryde to Freshwater route ran roughly parallel to the Central Chalk Ridge, across the very undulating northern lowlands. Upon reaching Yarmouth the line joined the extremely short valley of the western River Yar to reach the terminus at Freshwater.

HISTORICAL BACKGROUND

The 4¼ mile Cowes & Newport Railway was opened on 16th June 1862 and was unusual in not carrying any goods traffic. The Ryde & Newport Railway commenced operation on 20th December 1875 and ran into a new shared station at Newport, both railways being managed by a joint committee.

The fourth island railway company to be formed was the curiously named Isle of Wight (Newport Junction) Railway which intended to link the existing Isle of Wight Railway Company's Ryde to Ventnor line at Sandown with Newport. The line was opened to within one mile of Newport on 1st February 1875 but the construction of two major bridges bankrupted the company. After four years delay, the line was eventually completed, details being shown on the accompanying map. The Official Receiver arranged for a joint committee of the C&N and R&N to operate the line, thus bringing the Isle of Wight Central Railway into being in 1887.

The Newport, Godshill and St. Lawrence Railway Co. constructed a branch from Merstone to St. Lawrence and arranged for the IWCR to operate it from the opening day, on 20th July 1897. On 1st June 1900, the extension was opened to Ventnor Town, which was more honestly renamed Ventnor West by the Southern Railway.

A railway with a much troubled history was the Freshwater, Yarmouth & Newport. Even before the line was opened (10th September 1888 for goods and 19th July 1889 for passengers) there was trouble with the contractors and the directors attempted to seize their locomotive. After lengthy negotiations, terms were agreed for IWCR to provide and operate the trains but in 1913 a dispute arose and the directors decided to purchase their own rolling stock (with help from the Great Central Railway) and build their own terminus at Newport (with resulting inconvenience to passengers). Their locomotives had to be repaired by the IWR at their Ryde Works, the IWCR charging £3 for the movement of the engines over their lines. The problem over the shared station was resolved the following year but erupted again ten years later. The directors refused to accept the £50,000

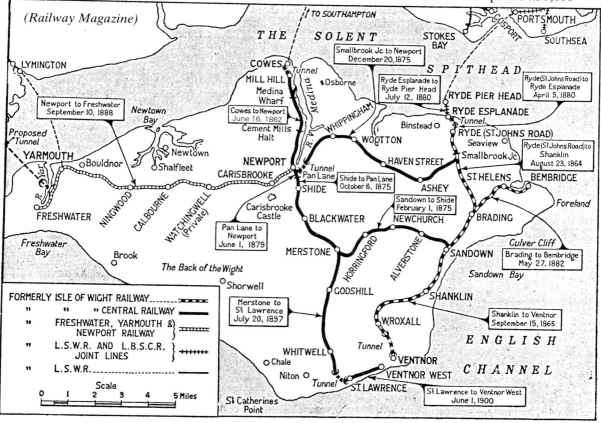

(Railway Magazine)

FORMERLY ISLE OF WIGHT RAILWAY
" " " CENTRAL RAILWAY
" FRESHWATER, YARMOUTH & NEWPORT RAILWAY
" L.S.W.R. AND L.B.S.C.R. JOINT LINES
" L.S.W.R.

Scale
0 1 2 3 4 5 Miles

offered for their railway when it was to be absorbed by the newly formed Southern Railway in January 1923. They demanded £70,000 and a counter offer of £60,000 was refused. At arbitration an award of £50,000 was made and during the eight month interval passengers were again subjected to the trouble of separate stations at Newport.

The other island lines voluntarily became part of the Southern Railway and the whole system benefited from an extensive programme of modernisation, albeit with largely secondhand mainland equipment. In January 1948 nationalisation brought the British Railway's emblems onto the Island but few other significant operational changes occurred until closures began – Ventnor West branch on 13th September 1952, the Freshwater line on 21st September 1953 and the Newport - Sandown route on 6th February 1956. The Cowes to Ryde passenger service was withdrawn on 21st February 1966, thus completely closing the 28¾ miles of the former IWCR and the 12 miles of the FYNR, the subjects of this album.

Revival of the Cowes to Newport line was considered in 1967-70 by Vectrail, using a Sadler Rail Coach (see picture 39 in our *Branch Lines to Alton*). A further scheme was put forward in 1976 for a three mile line of 15″ gauge track to be laid on the former track bed. The only preservation scheme to succeed was one that set out to preserve just a locomotive and finished up by opening a successful tourist line from Haven Street towards Wootton in 1972. Current plans envisage reopening to Smallbrook Junction, where an exchange platform with British Rail would be provided.

COWES, NEWPORT, MERSTONE, VENTNOR WEST, SANDOWN, and VENTNOR.

ISLE OF WIGHT & NEWPORT JUNCTION RAILWAYS.

:-o-:

MARKET TRAINS

FOR THE

WORKING CLASSES.

EVERY SATURDAY EVENING

(UNTIL FURTHER NOTICE)

CHEAP MARKET TICKETS

WILL BE ISSUED TO THE

WORKING CLASSES BY THE UNDERMENTIONED TRAINS,

At the following low rates :—

TO NEWPORT: via SANDOWN from					By Trains leaving at	Return Fares.
						s. d.
Ventnor..	..	..	..	..	5 25 p.m.	1 6
Wroxall	..	..	..	..	5 31 ,,	1 3
Shanklin	..	..	..	..	5 38 ,,	1 0
Ryde ..	..	..	..	..	5 30 ,,	1 2
Brading	..	..	..	..	5 38 ,,	1 0
Sandown	..	..	..	..	5 45 ,,	0 9
Alverstone	..	..	..	..	*	0 6
Newchurch	..	..	.	..	*	} 0 4
Horringford	..	..	.	..	*	}
Merstone	..	..	..	..	*	}
Blackwater	..	..	..	..	*	} 0 3
Shide ..	..	..	..	..	6 0 ...,,	}

Available to Return by the 8.40 p.m. Train from Newport.

* The 5.45 p.m. Train from Sandown will stop at these Stations by Signal to take up passengers.

These Tickets are available only between the Stations marked thereon.

IWR 1878 guide book.

PASSENGER SERVICES

The initial service on both the Cowes & Newport and the Ryde & Newport Railways was seven trains each way, with slightly fewer on Sundays. By 1925, the frequency on the former line had risen to 27 and on the latter there were 14 return journeys. Within a decade there were an additional 10 on each route, this being about the maximum ever provided. There was a reduction during World War II but a good service was maintained, principally to carry workers to the many factories at Cowes engaged in war work.

The incomplete route from Sandown to Pan Lane, Newport, had nine trains each way but this was soon reduced to seven after the line was finished. Eventually the earlier frequency was restored and reached a maximum of 15 between the wars.

The Ventnor West branch received seven weekday journeys in its early years, reaching as many as 12 in the 1930s.

The Freshwater line started with 11 trains on weekdays, this being reduced to 7 - 9 in the Edwardian period. Some trains ran through to Ryde until the break with the IWCR in 1913, but were resumed 20 years later.

In the summer of 1932, the *East and West Through Train* was run between Shanklin and Freshwater, complete with an observation car. For the following season it was extended to Ventnor and renamed *The Tourist*. Apart from the war years, this summer service operated until 1953 and was regarded by many as the finest journey on the Island.

COWES, NEWPORT, MERSTONE, VENTNOR WEST, SANDOWN, and VENTNOR

A Godshill Halt for Sandford (1¼ miles). B Whitwell Halt for Niton (1¼ miles) and Chale (4¼ miles). C St. Lawrence Halt for Blackgang (3¼ miles). D Nearest Sta. to Osborne House (by Ferry to East Cowes, thence Southern Vectis Bus). F Sta. for Brighstone.

LOCAL TRAINS between Newport and Cowes, page 180—Sandown and Ventnor, 180

1942

1. Cowes – Newport

COWES

1. The Cowes & Newport Railway's engine and carriage sheds were at Cowes, there being no such facilities at Newport initially. Here we see their condition after being damaged by a freak whirlwind in 1876. (T.P. Cooper collection)

2. This April 1936 view of the terminus shows the Terrier *Newport*, built by the LBSCR in 1878, running as Southern Railway no. W11 on a Sandown train. The locomotive had been purchased by the IWCR in 1902 and ran as their no.11. Her complicated life story before her recent return to the Isle of Wight Steam Railway is told in our *Branch Line to Hayling* under her original number – 40. The footbridge carried a public right of way and did not link the platforms. It replaced an earlier level crossing. (S.W. Baker)

3. The original terminus had been a wooden structure and it also housed the headquarters of the railway. The offices were moved to Newport in 1891. Being situated on the side of a hill, the station was inconvenient for ferry passengers, particularly if they had luggage to drag up the steps. A gate for parcel traffic was provided at platform level, further up Terminus Road on the right. (H.C. Casserley)

4. No.1 road, on the left, alone coped with normal services. No.2 was used for parcel traffic and for passengers on busy Saturdays. By 1965, only the 7.26am departure used no.3 (off the picture on the right) as the train was stabled there overnight. (Pamlin Prints)

COWES and NEWPORT.

Sec., Edward Lincoln, 2, Winchester Buildings, E.C.   Eng., H. Martin.

Cowes to Newport, at a6½, 9, and 10½ mrn.; 12½, 2½, 3½, 5½, 7½, and 59½ aft.   SUNDAYS at 9½ and 10 mrn.; 2½, 3½, 6½, and a8 30 aft.

Newport to Cowes at a6½, 9 20, and 11½ mrn.; 1, 2½, 4½, 6, 7½, and 59½ aft.   SUNDAYS at 9½ and 10½ mrn.; 2½, 3½, 6½, and a8½ aft.

☞ Through Tickets issued by Rail and Coach to and from Ventnor and Cowes.

FARES.—1s.; 9d.; 6d.; 4d.   RETURN, 1s. 6d.; 1s. 2d.

a Gov. b 3rd class; all others 1&2 class only.

Bradshaw 1869.

5. The spacious concourse was a pleasant affair with a generously glazed roof and sometimes hanging baskets of flowers, as seen here in 1964. Coaches were regularly gravitated down into the platform, usually successfully, but on 7th September 1889 five carriages for the 2.40pm departure scattered the waiting passengers and came to rest at the top of the steps to the street. (R.B. Owen)

6. The signal box had 22 levers and was a particularly busy place on the Friday of Regatta Week prior to WWII. Over 5000 passengers from all parts of the Island would arrive and depart during the evening, as it was Illuminations and Fireworks night. (J. Scrace)

7. The 1965 panorama from Granville Bridge includes two coal wharves on the left. On one occasion there was a points failure and passenger trains departed from the coal road. (J. Scrace)

1909 working timetable.

DOWN.		1	2	3	4	5	6	7	8	9	10	11	12
		Mail	Mixed	Pass.	Pass.	Pass.	Pass.	Pass.	Pass.	Pass.	Pass.	Pass	Pass.
Miles		a.m.	a.m.	a.m.	a.m.	a.m.	p.m.	p.m.	p.m.	p.m.	p.m.	p.m.	p.m.
	NEWPORT dep	5 10	8 15	9 5	11 5	11 26	1 5	3 10	4 30	5 15	6 40	8 0	9 15
1½	Cement Mills B	—	8 19	9 9	—	11 29	—	3 13	4 34	—	6 44	—	9 19
3	Medina Wharf pass	5 19	8 23	9 13	11 11	11 33	1 13	3 17	4 39	5 22	6 47	8 8	9 23
4	Mill Hill dep	—	8 28	9 18	—	11 38	1 18	3 22	4 43	5 26	6 53	8 12	9 27
4½	COWES arr	5 25	8 30	9 20	11 15	11 40	1 20	3 25	4 45	5 28	6 55	8 15	9 30

Wharf Engine to work as required.   N.B.—No Trains must cross at Medina Wharf in either direction by 5-30 a.m.   No. 5, 6, & 9 Week-days must run to time.   No. 6 not cal at Mills.
ELECTRIC TABLET. Newport, Medina Wharf, Cowes.

UP.		1	2	3	4	5	6	7	8	9	10	11	12	13
		Pass.	Pass.	Pass.	Pass.	Pass.	Exprs	Pass.	Pass.	Goods	Mixed	Mail	Pass.	Pass
Miles		a.m.	a.m.	a.m.	p.m.	p.m.	p.m.	p.m.	p.m.	p.m.	p.m.	p.m.	p.m. (Sats. excepted)	p.m. (Sats. only)
	COWES dep	8 45	10 0	11 45	12 40	2 50	3 35	5 5	5 31	...	7 40	8 30	9 45	10 0
¾	Mill Hill dep	8 47	10 2	11 B47	12 42	2 52	3 37	5 7	5 33	...	7 42	8 B32	9 47	10 2
1½	Medina Wharf pass	8 51	10 7	11 49	12 47	2 57	3 41	5 10	5 36	6 0	7 46	8 36	9 52	10 7
2½	Cement Mills B	8 54	10 11	—	12 51	3 0	—	—	5 40	6 15	7 49	—	9 56	10 11
4½	NEWPORT arr	8 58	10 15	11 56	12 55	3 5	3 47	5 15	5 43	6 30	7 55	8 42	10 0	10 15

No. 4. must run to time.
A. Saturdays only and other days at Station Master's discretion.
B. Calls by signal.   No. 13 must connect with Southampton Boat.

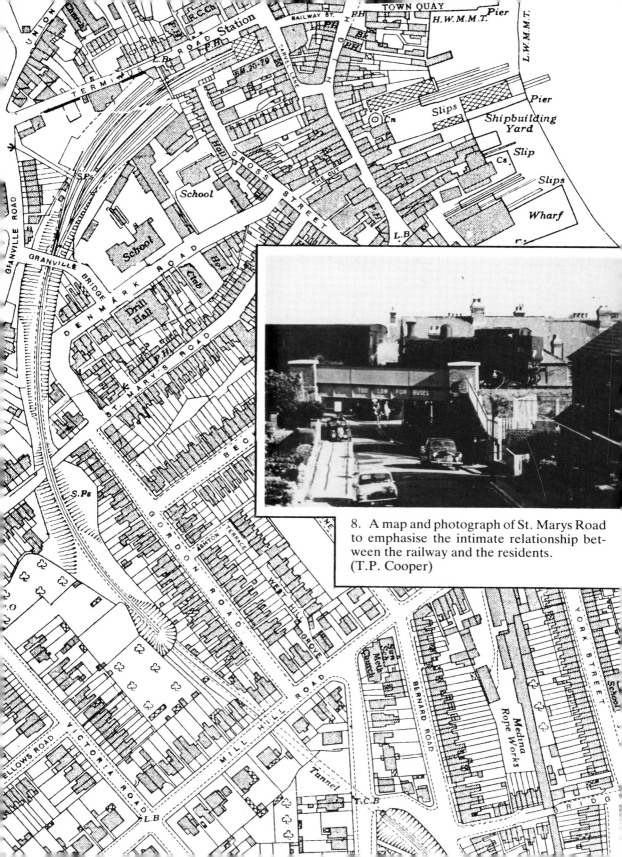

8. A map and photograph of St. Marys Road to emphasise the intimate relationship between the railway and the residents. (T.P. Cooper)

MILL HILL

9. Looking north towards the 208yd tunnel in the 1930s, we see the 1880 station building. The original wooden building, provided in 1871, was destroyed by fire in 1879. (WLS/AB McLeod)

10. No.32 drifts in with the normal summer rake of four coaches on the 11.18 from Ryde, on 19th September 1964. No goods facilities were available here but a heavy traffic of workers was handled on weekdays. (E. Wilmshurst)

11. The old gasworks had its own deep water wharf for colliers and a siding for the despatch of coke. This was situated on the far side of Smithards Lane crossing cottage, seen here from the north displaying its record-seeking chimney pot. (Pamlin Prints)

12. The main gates were always kept closed against the roadway despite generations of objectors. The reason for this was that the railway had only been required to provide an occupation crossing on farmland when the line was opened. Other historical facts – the crossing keeper's grandchild was killed on the crossing in 1887 – iron gates were provided in 1907. (D. Richardson)

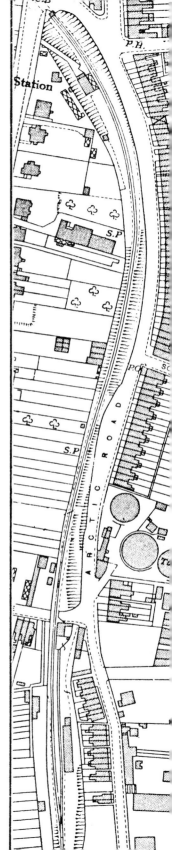

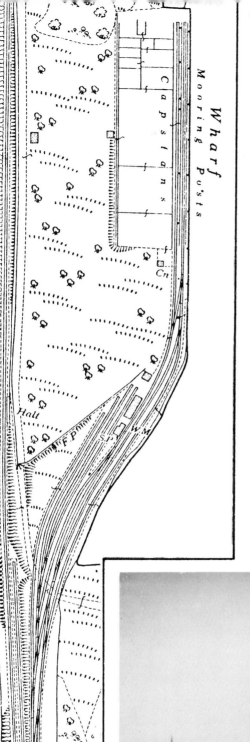

MEDINA WHARF

The gas holders of the former West Cowes Corporation Gas Works are shown as circles and the gasworks siding is seen south of the crossing. After the works closed the siding continued to be used by a local coal merchant (Woods). The distance from Medina Wharf was under ½ mile which must make this one of the shortest freight hauls anywhere.

13. A timber pier parallel to the shore and carrying two sidings was built in 1877-78. This was superseded by a substantial concrete structure in 1928. It carried two massive transporter cranes, each with grabs of 1½ ton capacity. After WWII, about 140,000 tons of coal was removed annually by rail, there being no road access whatsoever. Coaches and locomotives for the modernisation scheme were regularly landed at the wharf, having crossed from Southampton on the deck of the SR's own floating crane, hauled by 2 or 3 tugs. Here they are seen pushing their load up to the old wooden pier. (D. Cullum collection)

14. At the grouping of the railways in 1923, there were over 500 wagons on the Island's 50 or so miles of railway! This 1957 photograph shows that many of them could be found resting in the wharf sidings at any one time and that none were of the steel construction, by then common on the mainland. (H.C. Casserley)

15. A gradient of 1 in 60 led up to the main line, beyond the roadway on which a boy can be seen cycling. The train is the 12.30 Ryde to Cowes, hauled by no.22 on 9th August 1963. (E. Wilmshurst.

16. The wharf continued to be used by the engineers' department for some months after cessation of regular services. Here we see Gubbins & Ball's crane reuniting a wagon body with its wheels on 10th August 1966. By then there was a substantial road down to the waterfront. (A.E. Bennett)

17. For workers at the wharf who did not travel there on foot or bicycle, this staff halt was provided. It was a mere 43ft long and its location can be seen on the map.
(R. Silsbury collection)

1890

Fares frm Ryde (St. John's Rd.)	Down.	1,2,3	1&2	1&2	1&2	1&2	1&2	1&2	1&2	1&2	1&2	1&2	1&2	1,2,3	1&2	1&2	1&2	1&2
	44 WATERLOO (v.StksB)d		5 50		8 5		1115		2 20						1015			1 10
	52 „ (v.Portsmth)			6 45		9 30	1135		1245	4 10					9 3			1 10
	68 VICTORIA „			6 35		1030	1135		1 45	3 55					9 3			1 10
	68 LONDON BDG. „			6 45		1025	1140		1 50	4 55					8 55			1 20

CEMENT MILLS

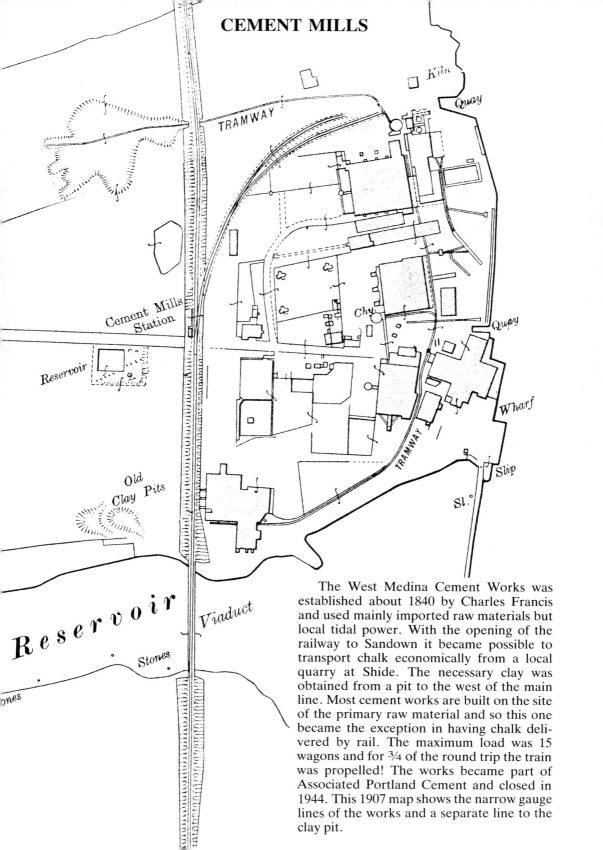

The West Medina Cement Works was established about 1840 by Charles Francis and used mainly imported raw materials but local tidal power. With the opening of the railway to Sandown it became possible to transport chalk economically from a local quarry at Shide. The necessary clay was obtained from a pit to the west of the main line. Most cement works are built on the site of the primary raw material and so this one became the exception in having chalk delivered by rail. The maximum load was 15 wagons and for ¾ of the round trip the train was propelled! The works became part of Associated Portland Cement and closed in 1944. This 1907 map shows the narrow gauge lines of the works and a separate line to the clay pit.

18. The sidings were laid with light weight rail and so were restricted for use by Terrier class locomotives only. The halt was originally provided for cement workers but after the works closed it remained as an unadvertised request stop, used mainly by fishermen. (Lens of Sutton)

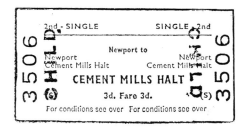

20. Those who can remember travelling on the line will be surprised to learn that officially there was a 10mph speed restriction on Mill Pond bridge. A Ryde-bound train rumbles over the reeds, three days before closure. (A.E. Bennett)

19. On 21st July 1924, the 4.04pm train from Cowes, hauled by 2–4–0 tank *Ventnor*, was in collision with a lorry loaded with cement. The SR thus obtained an all white train and a threat of legal proceedings. The railway's solicitor, however, discovered that the lorry was grossly overloaded and that its driver had no licence. (R. Silsbury collection)

Station

LittleLondon

NEWPORT
(Detached)

S.P.

F.P.

RIVER MEDINA

Station

Little London

24
1.399

B.S.

F.W.

F.F.

Co.Police
Office &
Bridewell

Inn

Gason

Ga

THE QUAY

N O R T H

SEA

W

E R   M E D I N A

CEMET

BLACKHOUSE LANE

S.B.
S.P.

S.P.

Engine
Shed

R
ation

Goods Yd.

Electricity
Works

HILLSIDE

Stone

W A R

Police
Station

LITTLE
LONDON

Quay

Cr

Cr

Quay

Gas
Works

Foundry

P.H.

Swing
Bridge

Cr

Quay
Slip

S.B.

S E A

H

NEWPORT

The top map is the 1874 edition, showing the basic terminus of the Cowes & Newport Railway and a narrow bridge over a tributary of the Medina leading to a steeply inclined station approach. The main map, from 1908, reveals a little known siding into the electricity works which had previously continued down an incline, of about 1 in 40, and crossed the river on a low level drawbridge. Its centre support is shown on the north side of the high level double track bridge. On reaching the west quay, it terminated on a wagon turntable from which double track ran along the waterfront. SB marks the position of the two signal boxes and SP the signal posts.

21. No.1 was built by Slaughter, Grüning & Co and was landed on the Medina mud flats at Medham Hard on 24th September 1861. It was appropriately named *Pioneer* and was scrapped in 1904. The drum on the boiler was a sand pot, the steam dome being obscured by the cab. The locomotive shed and works was opened in 1891 and was lit by open gas jets, visible by the cab roof.
(R.B. Owen collection)

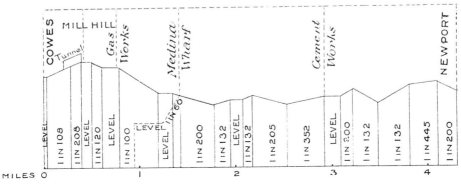

22. IWCR no.7 was acquired in 1908 from the Midland & South Western Junction Railway and was scrapped in 1926. The bulbous duckets gave the guard a good view of his train of four-wheelers hopping and swaying along the poorly laid track in the early 1920s, before the SR carried out its improvements. (Lens of Sutton)

23. The Cowes & Newport Railway only had three locomotives. This was their no.3, an 1870 Black Hawthorn, which was used latterly for shunting, mainly at Medina Wharf. On the down line is one of the five FYNR cattle wagons, which were open wagons fitted with corrugated iron roofs. (National Railway Museum)

24. The now famous Terrier no.11, seen earlier at Cowes, heads a train from Sandown in 1910. Note the South signal box beyond the loop platform and the ballast over the sleepers, a practice disapproved of on the mainland many years earlier. It could conceal defective timbers. (Lens of Sutton)

←

25. An unusually long train of assorted coaches leaves for Cowes, hauled by the elegant 4–4–0T no.6 and a 2–4–0T. The sidings on the left were often used for marshalling coal trains for different destinations on the Island when the Medina Wharf lines were congested. (R. Silsbury collection)

←

26. Soon after taking control, the SR introduced a number of ex-LSWR class O2 0–4–4Ts displaced by electrification of the suburban services from Waterloo. Here we see no.29 on a train for Sandown whilst another is standing in the Freshwater bay, on 23rd July 1935. (S.W. Baker)

27. In 1932-33, the SR introduced four class E1 tanks to operate the heavy coal trains. They were numbered 1 to 4. This is no.2 *Yarmouth*, built in 1880 as LBSCR no.152 *Hungary*. (S.W. Baker)

28. When BR was formed in 1948, there were three classes of locomotive on the Island – O2, E1 and A1X Terriers. The following year it was decided to try an E4. The experiment was a failure as the 57 ton monster collided with some of the platforms and was uneconomic on the trains it did run. Visiting no.2150 was photographed with resident no.W32. (S.C. Nash)

29. In latter years, loco crews had little time to admire the fine cast iron tracery of the water tank stanchion brackets or indeed clean more than just the number. The afternoon sun in September 1953 illuminates the air brake equipment clearly – the steam pump on the cab side and the reservoir under the bunker. (J.H. Aston)

30. The air cylinder is more obvious on O2 class no.20, as she hurries off to Cowes on 13th November 1965. Locomotive repair work was transferred to Ryde in about 1924, the shed subsequently being used for carriage repairs and painting. (S.C. Nash)

Part of S.W. Baker's observations on the morning of 14th September 1937.

FROM	LOCO.	TIME		LOCO.	TO
FRESHWATER	W.28	ARR 10.19			
RYDE	W.18	.20			
		.21	DEP	W.29	FRESHWATER
		.37		W.33	COWES
		.39		W.18	RYDE
SANDOWN	W.3	.41			
		.42		W.28	FRESHWATER
RYDE		11.6			
COWES	W.33	.7			
		.8		W.33	SANDOWN
		.8		W.19	COWES
SANDOWN		.35			
COWES	W.19	.37			
		.38		W.19	RYDE
FRESHWATER	W.29	12.5			
RYDE	W.14	.6			
		.8		W.14	COWES
		.9			SANDOWN
		.10		W.31	FRESHWATER
SANDOWN	W.33	.35			
COWES	W.14	.37			
		.38		W.14	RYDE
		.38		W.33	COWES
FRESHWATER	W.28	.57			
RYDE	W.21	1.6			
COWES	W.33	.7			

31. With signal arms removed, locomotives and coaches await scrapping, nearly a year after closure. Further views of Newport in happier times appear in pictures 49 - 55 and 115 - 123. (S.C. Nash)

32. This is the scene at the Cowes end of platform 2 on 1st November 1969, when all the other locomotives and most of the coaches had been scrapped. Wight Locomotive Society volunteers work on, with their future uncertain. With two weeks notice to vacate the site, they steamed off to Haven Street on 24th January 1971. (J.A.M. Vaughan)

1909 working timetable.

2. Smallbrook J. – Newport

SMALLBROOK JUNCTION

33. Until 1926 there was no junction at this location, the IWCR line from Cowes (on the right) running parallel to IWR line from Ventnor as far as Ryde St. Johns Road. The SR built this small signal box and installed the junction so that the two single tracks could be used as double track, at least in the summer. Pictures 51 and 52 in our *Ryde to Ventnor* album complete the story. (J. Scrace)

UP. **WEEK-DAYS.**

Miles			1	2	3	4	5	6	7	8	9	10	11	12	13	14
			Mail En (Mondays only)	Mail En (Mondays excepted)	Mixed	Pass	Mixed	Lt. En	Mxd	Pass	Pass	Pass	LtEn.	Mixed	Mail	Pass (Satdys only)
			a.m.	a.m.	a.m.	a.m.	a.m.	noon	p.m	p.m	p.m	p.m.	p.m.	p.m.	p.m.	p.m
	NEWPORT	dep	2 30		7 25	9 25	10 25		1 10	3 10	5 0	5 45		8 0	8 45	9 15
2¼	Whippingham	A	pass.		7 30	9 31	10 31	–	1 15	3 15	5 5	5 ps 49		8 6	8ps49	9 20
3	Wootton	dep			7 33	9 34	10 34	–	1 18	3 18	5 8	5 52		8 10	8A51	9 24
4½	Haven Street	A			7 38	9 40	10 39	–	1 24	3 22	5 12	5 ps 55		8 16	8ps54	9 28
6	Ashey	A	2 45		7 43	9 43	10B44	–	1 28	3 26	5 16	5 ps 58		8E22	8ps57	9 33
8½	Ryde (St. John's Rd.)	arr	–		7 48	9 48	10 50		1 33	3 32	5 22	6 C 3		8 29	9 3	9 40
8½	Ryde (St. John's Rd.)	dep	2 55	2 30	7 50	9 49	10 51	12 10	1 34	3 33	5 23	6 5	7 55	8 30	9 4	
9	Ryde (Esplanade)	dep	2 58	2 33	7 54	9 52	10 53	12 13	1 37	3 37	5 27	6 8	7 58	8 32	9 7	—
9¾	RYDE (Pier Head)	arr	3 0	2 35	7 56	9 55	10 55	12 15	1 40	3 40	5 30	6 10	8 0	8 35	9 10	—

A Calls by Signal. B Cross No. 3 Down. C Cross No. 8 Down. E Cross No. 10 Down.

NOTES. Week-days. – No. 3 Must run to time to prevent delay to London Services.

Nos. 5, 7 & 12 Not more than one spring buffered wagon, with screw coupling, must be attached to these Trains without special authority. No intermediate Sidings to be worked unless ordered.

No. 14 Cross No. 11 Down at Ashey.

Ryde Goods Trains to run as per notice between 6 a.m. and 7 a.m.

ELECTRIC BLOCK. Newport, Wootton, Ashey.

DOWN. **WEEK-DAYS.**

Miles			1	2	3	4	5	6	7	8	9	10	11	12	13
			Mail	Pass	Pass.	Lt. En	Mixed	Pass	Pass.	Pass.	Lt. En	Pass	Emp.	Mail En.	Pass. (Saturdays only)
			a.m.	a.m.	a.m.	a.m.	noon	p.m.	p.m	p.m.	p.m.	p.m	p.m.	p.m.	p.m.
	RYDE (Pier Head)	dep	3 25	8 20	10 30	11 5	12 20	2 35	3 50	6 0	6 25	8 5	8 35	9 20	
½	Ryde (Esplanade)	dep	3 30	8 22	10 32	11 7	12 22	2 37	3 52	6 2	6 27	8 7	8 37	9 22	
1¼	Ryde (St. John's Rd.)	arr	3 33	8 24	10 34	11 10	12 24	2 39	3 54	6 5	6 30	8 9	8 40	9 25	
													Goods		
1¼	Ryde (St. John's Rd.)	dep	3D35	8 30	10 37	Shunt Ryde Yard.	12 30	2 44	3 59	6C10	Shunt Ryde Yard	8 14	9 30		9 45
3¾	Ashey	A	3E43	8 38	10B44		12 38	2 50	4 5	6 18		8G22	9 40		9 52
5	Haven Street	A	pass	8 42	10 48		12 42	2 54	4 9	6 22		8 26	9 45		9 56
6½	Wootton	dep	pass	8 46	10 53		12 47	2 58	4 13	6 27		8 31	9 55		10A1
7½	Whippingham	A	3F55	8 49	10 55		12 50	3 0	4 15	6 30		8 34	10 0		10 4
9¾	NEWPORT	arr	4 0	8 55	11 0		12 55	3 5	4 20	6 35		8 40	10 10		10 10

A. Calls by Signal. B. Cross No 5 Up unless late. C. Cross No. 10 Up at St. John's Road.

NOTES. – Week-days.

No. 11 cross No. 14 Up at Ashey.

No. 1 D–Arrive on I. W. R. Road, cross over and pick up Tablet. E–Tablet and Staff. F–Stop for Bridge Test.

ASHEY

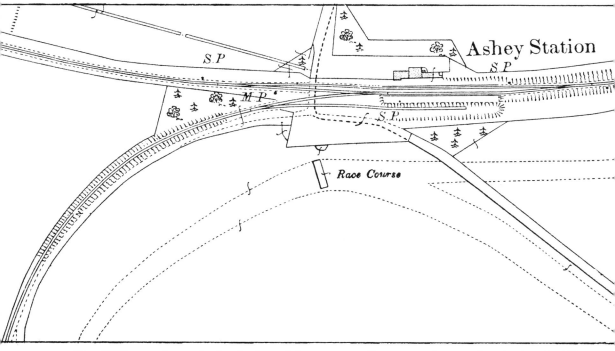

The 1908 map shows the beginning of the ½ mile long branch to a chalk quarry on Ashey Down. Material from it was used in the construction of the main line. At the quarry there was a locomotive shed and a 40ft tunnel, which took the line under a road. It was not used after WWI but part of the line remained for stabling race trains.

34. Ashey Races were usually held twice a year and as many as 3000 people a day would arrive by train. The train clad with spectators appears to be standing in the loop and not the siding. Trains berthed on the quarry line were also used as temporary refreshment rooms. (R. Brinton collection)

35. The 10-lever signal box was normally opened only on race days and the small shunt signal seen on the post was used equally infrequently. Racing ceased in 1929 after the grandstand had been destroyed by fire. (R. Brinton collection)

36. In 1926 the loop was reduced to a siding, and the little used station became an unstaffed halt in 1953, the year in which this photograph was taken. The lavish architectural style was for the benefit of Sir Henry Oglander, a local landowner, and the building survives today, in use as a dwelling. (J.H. Aston)

37. Owing to ground movement, the track was slewed over to the down platform in 1961 and a small waiting shelter was erected thereon. The up platform name board had previously assumed an angle similar to that of the trespassers warning in this view, due to the mobile clay. (J. Scrace)

38. Another view in the last summer of operation, shows no.35 accelerating away towards Newport; the second coach is passing over the foot crossing. In 1949, a survey had revealed an average of 12 passengers using the station daily in the winter and 20 in the summer. (S.C. Nash)

HAVEN STREET

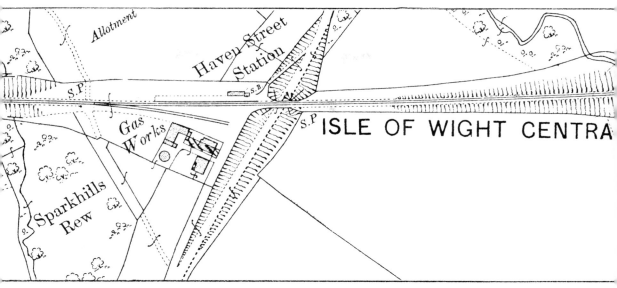

39. The improved train service to Cowes introduced in 1926 necessitated the construction of a passing loop here. No.18 awaits the arrival of a westbound train, in September 1946. The fine row of platform lamps reminds us that the station was totally oil lit until 1977. (S.W. Baker)

The 1908 map shows the position of the small wooden station buildings, insignificant when compared with Ashey. The gasworks was built by the local landowner, Mr. John Rylands, in 1886 and it provided some railway traffic until the 1920s.

40. No.28 drifts in with a Cowes train on 7th September 1953, past the deserted goods yard. The siding ground signal is adjacent to its catch point. (P. Hay)

41. This 1965 view from the top of the down home signal shows the well kept footpath from the village, the lack of a siding at that time and the considerable deviation of the up loop from the old direct line. (J. Scrace)

42. The new red brick station provided in 1926 was unusual in being connected to the island platform by a mere foot crossing. A 16-lever knee frame was installed in the projecting part of the building. The seat on the right was the annual trophy in the "Best kept station competition" on the Island. It often came to rest here for a year and now resides there in the museum. (J.A.M. Vaughan)

43. It is impossible to do justice to the tremendous achievements of the volunteer members of the Isle of Wight Steam Railway in one paragraph. Readers not familiar with the beautifully restored Island rolling stock can only be recommended to see it in action one summer Sunday. Here no.8 *Freshwater* blows off before the TV camera on the occasion of the launch of the companion album to this on 21st July 1985. (V. Mitchell)

WOOTTON

44. The entrance to the station was by the upper lamp post and the booking office, together with the waiting room, was economically located in a bridge arch.
(D. Cullum collection)

The 1908 map indicates one siding (used mainly for coal) and one chapel (now one of two Methodist Chapels in Wootton). Otherwise there were only occasional cottages before reaching the village centre ½ mile away.

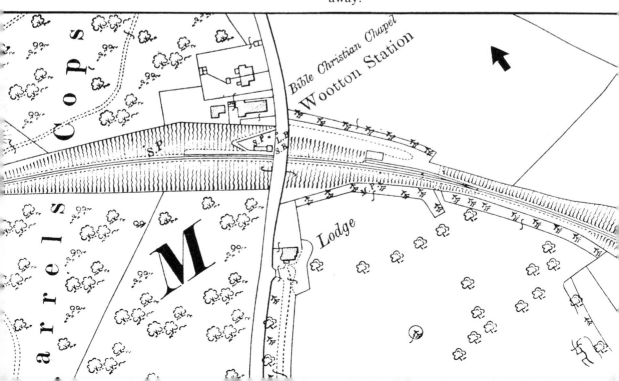

45. The "Best Kept Station" seat is seen here, two weeks before the station was closed on 21st September 1953. Shortly afterwards, the platform was removed as it was creeping too close to the track, again due to unstable clay sub soil. By 1971, the track was so distorted that the preserved stock on its way from Newport to Haven Street passed at great peril. The cutting is now filled in. (P. Hay)

46. The Isle of Wight Steam Railway laid a loop and engineers' siding but the passenger platform was not opened until 31st May 1987. The former Freshwater signal box contains eight levers from the old Shanklin frame. No. 8 is another Terrier with an unusual history described in *Branch Line to Hayling*, under its LBSCR number – 46. (V. Mitchell)

WHIPPINGHAM

47. A mirror image of Ashey station in the same opulent style, the station was intended for the use of Queen Victoria when visiting Osborne House. Eventually it was made available to local residents – not that there were ever very many – even now, the nearest building is the crematorium.
(R. Silsbury collection)

48. In 1912, a loop was installed and the down platform on the right was built with a summerhouse-like waiting shelter on it. The station was closed on 21st September 1953 and all trains ran through on the down line although the loop remained usable until 1956. Coaches are standing in the only siding provided. (WLS/AB McLeod)

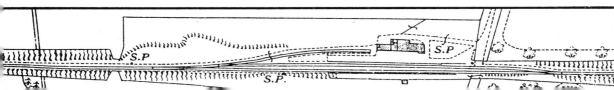

NEWPORT

49. With check rails everywhere, we view the divergence of the lines, from the drawbridge. On the left is the Ryde line and on the right, the route to Sandown. Beyond the arches was a lengthy lattice girder bridge – Coppins bridge. This structure contributed to bankrupting the original company; had to be rebuilt in 1920; was demolished in 1960 and is now the site of a major new road system which includes a highway on the trackbed to Shide. (Pamlin Prints)

1910

Offices—Newport, I.W.] RYDE, NEWPORT, VENTNOR, and COWES.—Isle of Wight Central. [Gen. Man., Chas. L. Conacher.

Miles from Ryde (P. H.)	Down.	Week Days. gov	mrn	mrn	mrn	mrn	mrn	mrn	aft	aft	aft	aft	aft	aft	aft	aft	af			Sundays. mrn	mrn	mrn	aft	mrn	aft	aft	aft
	126 Waterloo * ..dep.	....	....	....	....	....	....	....	....	....	....	....	....	....	....	....	....	....	....	....	....	....	....	....	....	....	....
	126 " † 138 "	....	....	5 20	6 20	....	9 10	9 20	1245	....	2 20	....	4 55	....	....	....	....	....	....	....	....	8 40	....	10 0	....	....	....
	184 Victoria † ... "	....	....	....	6 20	....	....	1125	....	....	1 42	....	3 55	....	....	....	....	....	....	....	....	9 0	....	....	....	....	1 10
	184 London Bdg. † "	....	....	....	6 35	....	....	1120	....	....	1 50	....	4 50	....	....	....	....	....	....	....	....	8 55	....	....	....	....	1 10
—	Ryde (Pier Head)..dep.	....	8 20	9 15	1030	....	1220	2 35	3 50	....	6 0	....	8 5	Saturdays only.	....	9 10	....	....	....	....	1050	1 15	....	3 10	....	6 20	8 55
¼	" (Esplanade)......	....	8 22	9 20	1032	....	1222	2 37	3 52	....	6 2	....	8 7		....	9 13	....	....	....	....	1052	1 17	....	3 12	....	6 22	8 57
1¼	" (St. John's Road)	....	8 30	9 25	1037	....	1230	2 44	3 59	....	6 10	....	8 14		....	9 16	9 45	....	....	....	1057	1 22	....	3 18	....	6 28	9 5
3¼	Ashey, for Nunwell....	....	Sig.	Via Sandown.	Sig.	....	Sig.	Sig.	Sig.	....	Sig.	....	Sig.			....	Sig.	....	....	....	Sig.	Sig.	....	Sig.	....	Sig.	Sig.
5	Haven Street.........	....	Sig.		Sig.	....	Sig	Sig.	Sig.	....	Sig.	....	Sig.			....	Sig.	....	....	....	Sig.	Sig.	....	Sig.	....	Sig.	Sig.
6¼	Wootton..............	....	8 46		1053	....	1247	2 58	4 13	....	6 27	....	8 31		Saturdays only.		10 1	....	....	....	1112	1 38	....	3 32	....	6 44	9 20
7¼	Whippingham.........	....	Sig.		Sig.	. .	Sig.	Sig.	Sig.	....	Sig.	....	Sig.			Saturdays only. Via Sandown.	Sig.	....	....	....	Sig.	Sig.	....	Sig.	....	Sig.	Sig.
9¼	Newport..........arr.	....	8 55		11 0	....	1255	3 5	4 20	....	6 35	....	8 40				1010	....	....	....	1120	1 45	....	3 40	....	6 53	9 28
—	Newport......dep.	....	9 2		1130	....	1 10	3 15	4 35	....	6 40	....	....	9 15			Saturdays only.	....	....	....	1135	....	....	....	....	7 0	....
10¾	Carisbrooke ** [fleet	....	9 9		Sig.	....	1 17	Sig.	Sig.	....	6 47	....	....	Sig.				....	....	....	Sig.	....	....	....	....	7 7	....
15	Calbourne, for Shal-	....	9 19		Sig.	....	Sig.	Sig.	Sig.	....	Sig.	....	....	9 32				....	....	....	Sig.	....	....	....	....	7 17	....
16½	Ningwood........	....	9 23		Sig.	....	Sig.	Sig.	Sig.	....	Sig.	....	....	9 37				....	....	....	Sig.	....	....	....	....	7 21	....
19½	131 Yarmouth........	....	9 32		12 0	....	1 40	3 45	5 10	....	7 10	....	....	9 45				....	....	....	12 5	....	....	....	....	7 30	....
21½	Freshwater †† arr.	....	9 37		12 5	....	1 45	3 50	5 15	....	7 15	....	....	9 50				....	....	....	1210	....	....	....	....	7 35	....
—	Mls VentnorTown d	....	8 25	9 45	....	1055	1230	2 35	....	4 45	6 0	....	8 40	....	9 45			....	....	....	1035	....	....	....	....	....	9 0
—	1½ St. Lawrence § ..	....	Sig.	Sig.	....	Sig.	Sig.	Sig.	....	Sig.	Sig.	....	Sig.	....	Sig.			....	....	....	Sig.	....	....	....	....	....	Sig.
—	2½ Whitwell ‖	....	8 35	9 55	....	11 3	1238	2 43	....	4 53	6 8	....	8 48	....	9 53			....	....	....	1044	....	....	....	....	....	9 8
—	5¼ Godshill ¶	....	Sig.	Sig.	....	Sig.	Sig.	Sig.	....	Sig.	Sig.	....	Sig.	....	Sig.			....	....	....	Sig.	....	....	....	....	....	Sig.
—	6¾ Merstone Jn. arr	....	8 45	10 2	....	1119	1246	2 50	....	Sig.	6 15	....	8 55	....	10 0			....	....	....	1052	....	....	....	....	....	9 15
—	Mls Sandown Jnc. dep.	....	8 30	9 45	....	1055	1230	2 35	3 55	....	6 0	....	8 40	....	....	9 45	....	....	....	....	1035	....	2 15	....	4 40	....	9 0
—	1½ Alverstone.........	....	Sig.	....	....	Sig.	Sig.	Sig.	Sig.	....	Sig.	....	Sig.	....	....	Sig.	....	....	....	....	Sig.	....	Sig.	....	Sig.	....	Sig.
—	2½ Newchurch.........	....	Sig.	....	....	Sig.	Sig.	Sig.	Sig.	....	Sig.	....	Sig.	....	....	Sig.	....	....	....	....	Sig.	....	Sig.	....	Sig.	....	Sig.
—	3½ Horringford	....	Sig.	....	....	Sig.	Sig.	Sig.	Sig.	....	Sig.	....	Sig.	....	....	Sig.	....	....	....	....	Sig.	....	Sig.	....	Sig.	....	Sig.
—	5½ Merstone Junc. ar	....	8 45	10 3	....	11 9	1245	2 50	Sig.	....	6 17	....	8 55	....	....	10 0	....	....	....	....	1050	....	2 28	....	4 54	....	9 15
—	— Merstone Jnc. dep.	....	8 47	10 5	....	1112	1247	2 52	Sig.	5 0	6 18	....	8 58	....	....	10 3	....	....	....	...	1054	....	2 29	....	4 57	....	9 17
—	7 Blackwater	....	Sig.	....	....	Sig.	Sig.	Sig.	Sig.	Sig.	Sig.	....	Sig.	....	....	Sig.	....	....	....	....	Sig.	....	Sig.	....	Sig.	....	Sig.
—	8½ Shide	....	Sig.	....	....	Sig.	Sig.	Sig.	Sig.	Sig.	Sig.	....	Sig.	....	....	Sig.	....	....	....	....	Sig.	....	Sig.	....	Sig.	....	Sig.
—	9½ Newport .....arr.	....	8 58	1015	....	1124	1258	1 0	4 25	5 10	6 30	....	9 10	....	....	1015	....	....	....	....	11 5	....	2 39	....	5 8	....	9 28
—	Newport..........dep.	8 15	9 5	....	11 5	1126	1 5	3 10	4 30	5 15	6 40	8 0	9 15	....	....	....	....	....	....	9 35	1125	2 0	....	3 42	5 10	....	9 30
13¼	Mill Hill..............	8 28	9 18	....	....	1138	1 18	3 22	4 43	5 26	6 53	8 13	9 27	....	....	....	....	....	....	9 48	1137	2 11	....	3 53	5 23	....	9 43
14	Cowes ‡ 131......arr.	8 30	9 20	....	1115	1140	1 20	3 25	4 45	5 28	6 55	8 15	9 30	....	....	....	....	....	....	9 50	1140	2 13	....	3 55	5 25	....	9 45
105¼	131 Waterloo ¶¶ arr.	....	1 31	....	....	....	4 45	7 31	....	10 5	3b35	....	....	....	....	....	....	....	....	....	....	....	....	8 49	....	....	....

NOTES.

ƃ Sunday mornings.

* Via Stokes Bay.

† Via Portsmouth.

‡ Nearest Station to Osborne College (by Ferry to East Cowes.

§ Station for Blackgang (3½ miles).

‖ Station for Niton (1½ miles) and Chale (4½ miles).

¶ Station for Sandford (1½ miles).

** Station for Castle.

†† Station for Totland Bay (1½ miles), Alum Bay (2½ miles), and the Needles (3½ miles).

¶¶ Via Southampton.

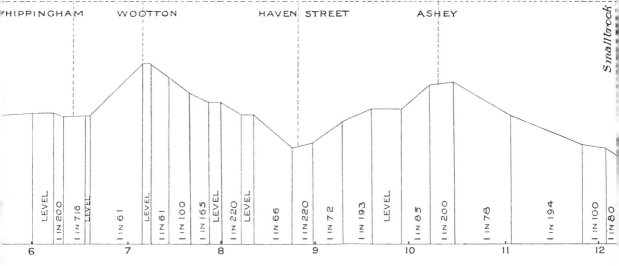

LEVEL 1 IN 200 1 IN 716 LEVEL 1 IN 61 LEVEL 1 IN 61 1 IN 100 1 IN 165 LEVEL 1 IN 220 LEVEL 1 IN 66 1 IN 220 1 IN 72 1 IN 193 LEVEL 1 IN 85 1 IN 200 1 IN 78 1 IN 194 1 IN 100 1 IN 80

6   7   8   9   10   11   12

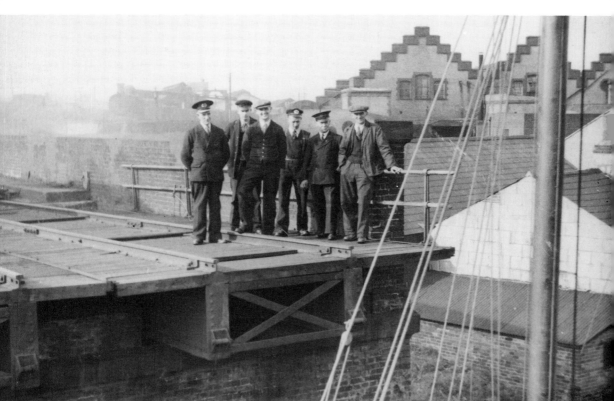

50. Three photographs taken on 21st March 1949 to show the Medina drawbridge in action. The staff rest for a few minutes as the mast of a passing vessel appears in the right of the picture. (R.C.J. Day)

52. The final operation was to replace the fishplates and reconnect the signal wires. Ships had priority over trains but on one occasion, a signal man delayed a vessel departing on a falling tide and it grounded between the abutments. Train services ceased until the next tide. (R.C.J. Day)

51. The moving spans were counterbalanced by weights hanging on chains. Here they are being wound back into position whilst the disconnected signal wires lay beside the handrails. Standing at the end of a siding in the background is the disgraced E4 tank and on the left is the South Box. (R.C.J. Day)

53. No.35 *Freshwater* arrives from Ryde on 8th April 1963, at which time only one draw-bridge remained, the other one having been dismantled soon after the closure of the Sandown line in 1956. After abolition of South Box an auxiliary key token instrument was installed at this end of the station, to avoid a long walk to North Box with the token. (S.J. Greenwood)

55. By November 1969, Newport turned its back on the station that had for so many years brought business and prosperity to the town. (J.A.M. Vaughan)

54. Looking north, three days before the withdrawal of services, we can observe the vacant plinths of the dismantled spans and also one of the supports for an earlier low-level drawbridge. On the right is the swing bridge for dockside traffic. (S.C. Nash)

3. Sandown – Shide

SANDOWN

56. Terrier no.11 rises up the 1 in 54 gradient from the Yar valley to the junction with the line from Ryde, which is on the extreme right. The wagons are standing on the siding to the brickworks, part of which is visible to the rear of the train. (D. Cullum collection)

57. To the south of the station building were the offices of the Isle of Wight Railway, for most of that company's life. This 1920 view remains basically unaltered today.
(D. Cullum collection)

58. The lofty signal box towers above the platform awning as E1 class no.2 *Yarmouth* arrives with a train from Newport. Ashey Down rises majestically in the background. A map and other views of this station appear in the *Ryde to Ventnor* album. (P. Hay)

Half a mile from Sandown, at the foot of the incline, a siding was provided for coal traffic to the waterworks.

SANDOWN to COWES.	WEEK DAYS.								
	1 2 3	1 & 2	1 & 2	1 & 2	1 & 2	1 & 2	1 & 2	1 & 2	1 & 2
	a.m.	a.m.	a.m.	p.m.	p.m.	p.m.	p.m.	p.m.	p.m.
(SA)NDOWN JUN. dep.	8 30	9 42	10 55	1 35	3 42	...	5 54	...	8 10 ...
(Hor)ringford .... ,,	8 42	9 54	11 7	1 47	3 54	...	6 6	Sats.	8 22 ...
(Shi)de .... ,,	8 56	10 8	11 21	2 1	4 8	...	6 20	...	8 36 ...
(NE)WPORT .... ,,	9 17	11 16	11 27	2 6	4 15	5 10	6 26	7 33	8 41 ...
(CO)WES .... arr.	9 30	11 31	11 42	2 21	4 30	5 23	6 41	7 48	8 56 ...

COWES to SANDOWN.	WEEK DAYS.								B
	1 2 3	1 & 2	1 & 2	1 & 2	1 & 2	1 & 2	1 & 2	1 & 2	1 & 2
	a.m.	a.m.	a.m.	p.m.	p.m.	p.m.	p.m.	p.m.	p.m.
COWES .... dep.	8 50	9 55	11 47	12 35	2 23	2 40	5 0	7 15	8 10
NEWPORT............ ,,	9 5	10 12	12 2	12 55	2 38	2 57	5 12	7 31	8 40
Shide .... ,,	9 9	10 16	...	12 59	...	3 1	5 15	7 35	8 43
Horringford .... ,,	9 23	10 30	...	1 11	...	3 15	5 29	7 49	8 57
SANDOWN JUNC. arr.	9 35	10 42	...	1 23	...	3 27	5 41	8 1	9 10

B Saturdays only.

Sundays Trains leave Sandown Junction for Newport at 10.30 a.m., 2.5, 4.30 and 8.50 p.m., and Newport for Sandown Junction 12.35 p.m. 2.40, 7.20 and 9.25

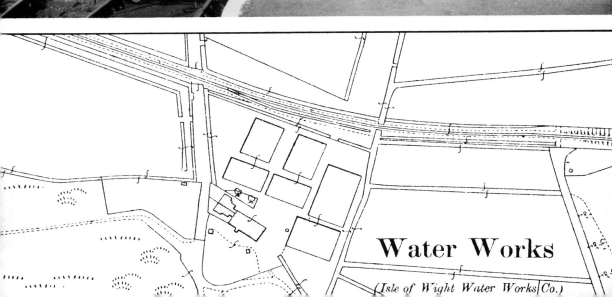

Water Works

(Isle of Wight Water Works Co.)

ALVERSTONE

59. The substantial building survives today as a house but is not the original structure. Note the St. John's Ambulance stretcher cupboard on the platform and the mill race on the left. This also passed under the single siding, whilst the mill stream ran to the right of the station. (A.W. Burges)

RYDE, NEWPORT, SANDOWN, VENTNOR WEST, and COWES—Southern (late Isle of Wight C

Mls	Down.		Week Days.																					
			mn	mrn	mrn	mn	mrn	mrn	mrn	mrn	mrn	mrn	aft	mrn	aft	mrn	mrn	mn	aft	aft	aft	aft	aft	aft
170	Waterloo 178	dep.	...	...	...	...	...	...	5U50	...	...	8H20	...	9s50	...	9F50	1150	U	12s50	V	1U50	...	2s50	...
	Ryde (Pier Head)	dep.	...	...	...	...	8 20	...	9 44	1044	...	1142	...	1242	...	1 42	2 42	...	3 42	...	4 42	...	5 42	...
	" (Esplanade)		...	...	...	...	8 23	...	9 47	1047	...	1145	...	1245	...	1 45	2 45	...	3 45	...	4 45	...	5 45	...
	" (St. John's Road)		...	...	...	...	8 26	...	9 50	1050	...	1148	...	1248	...	1 48	2 48	...	3 48	...	4 48	...	5 48	...
	Ashey		...	...	...	...	8 34	...	9 58	1058	...	1157	...	1257	...	1 57	2 57	...	3 57	...	4 57	...	5 57	...
	Haven Street		...	...	...	...	8 40	...	10 2	11 2	...	12 1	...	1 1	...	2 1	3 1	...	4 1	...	5 1	...	6 1	...
	Wootton		...	...	...	...	8 44	...	10 6	11 6	...	12 5	...	1 5	...	2 5	3 5	...	4 5	...	5 5	...	6 5	...
	Whippingham		...	...	...	...	8 47	...	10 9	11 9	...	12 8	...	1 8	...	2 8	3 8	...	4 8	...	5 8	...	6 8	...
	Newport 193, 195	arr.	...	...	...	...	8 52	...	1014	1114	...	1213	...	1 13	...	2 13	3 13	...	4 13	...	5 13	...	6 13	...
Mls	Sandown	dep.	...	...	...	...	8 24	...	9 44	1044	...	1144	...	1244	...	1 44	2 44	...	3 44	...	4 44	...	5 44	...
1¼	Alverstone		...	...	...	...	8 28	...	9 48	1048	...	1148	...	1248	...	1 48	2 48	...	3 48	...	4 48	...	5 48	...
2½	Newchurch		...	...	...	...	8 31	...	9 51	1051	...	1151	...	1251	...	1 51	2 51	...	3 51	...	4 51	...	5 51	...
3¾	Horringford		...	...	...	...	8 34	...	9 54	1054	...	1154	...	1254	...	1 54	2 54	...	3 54	...	4 54	...	5 54	...
5¼	Merstone 195	arr.	...	...	...	...	8 37	...	9 57	1057	...	1157	...	1257	...	1 57	2 57	...	3 57	...	4 57	...	5 57	...
Mls	Ventnor West	dep.	...	...	...	...	8 20	...	...	1038	...	1138	...	1238	...	...	2 38	...	3 38	...	4 38	...	5 38	...
1½	St. Lawrence †		...	...	...	...	8 24	...	...	1042	...	1142	...	1242	...	...	2 42	...	3 42	...	4 42	...	5 42	...
2¾	Whitwell ‡		...	...	...	...	8 28	...	...	1046	...	1146	...	1246	...	...	2 46	...	3 46	...	4 46	...	5 46	...
5¼	Godshill §		...	...	...	...	8 33	...	...	1052	...	1152	...	1252	...	...	2 52	...	3 52	...	4 52	...	5 52	...
6¾	Merstone 195	arr.	...	...	...	...	8 36	...	...	1055	...	1155	...	1255	...	...	2 55	...	3 55	...	4 55	...	5 55	...
—	Merstone	dep.	...	...	...	...	8 38	...	9 59	1059	...	1159	...	1259	...	1 59	2 59	...	3 59	...	4 59	...	5 59	...
7	Blackwater (Isle of W.)		...	...	...	...	8 42	...	10 3	11 3	...	12 3	...	1 3	...	2 3	3 3	...	4 3	...	5 3	...	6 3	...
8¼	Shide		...	...	...	...	8 46	...	10 7	11 7	...	12 7	...	1 7	...	2 7	3 7	...	4 7	...	5 7	...	6 7	...
9¼	Newport 193, 195	arr.	...	...	...	...	8 49	...	1010	1110	...	1210	...	1 10	...	2 10	3 10	...	4 10	...	5 10	...	6 10	...
	Newport	dep.	6 46	7 14	7 42	8 16	8 55	9 22	1018	1118	1146	1216	1246	1 16	1 46	2 16	3 16	3 46	4 16	4 46	5 16	5 46	6 16	6 4
	Mill Hill		6 54	7 22	7 50	8 24	9 3	9 30	1026	1126	1154	1224	1254	1 24	1 54	2 24	3 24	3 54	4 24	4 54	5 24	5 54	6 24	65
	Cowes ‖	arr.	6 56	7 24	7 52	8 26	9 5	9 32	1028	1128	1156	1226	1256	1 26	1 56	2 26	3 26	3 56	4 26	4 56	5 26	5 56	6 26	65
	Southampton ¶	arr.	...	9 0	...	...	1045	1045	...	...	...	...	...	2 45	...	...	4 45	...	...	...	...	7 25	...	...
152	Waterloo	"	...	11U0	...	U	1250	1250	U	...	...	...	...	4R50	...	...	6B58	...	...	...	B	1120	...	...

Colman's Withybed

F.P.

C.S.

F.B. St.

Corn Mill

S.P.

Station

S.P. Alverstone Bridge

NOTES.

A Leaves at 5 50 aft. on Saturdays. Dining Car except on Saturdays.
B Dining Car.
F Leaves at 10 50 mrn. on Saturdays.
H Breakfast Car.
R Restaurant Car.
S Saturdays only.
U Light Refreshments served.
V Luncheon Car.
† Station for Blackgang (3½ miles).
‡ Station for Niton (1½ mls) & Chale (4½ mls).
§ Station for Sandford (1½ miles).
‖ Nearest Station to Osborne College (by Ferry to East Cowes).
¶ By Boat. Passengers must make their own way between the Royal Pier and West Station at Southampton.

60. Class O2 no.18 *Ningwood* moves off towards Newchurch on 1st June 1953, with the lineside hay freshly cut. (P. Hay)

1924 SR timetable.

NEWCHURCH

61. The original cottage and station at Alverstone were similar to those illustrated here, but when these were demolished, no replacement dwelling was provided, only a wooden shed on the platform. This contained a waiting area, a booking office and a 10-lever frame, the station being an intermediate block post. (Lens of Sutton)

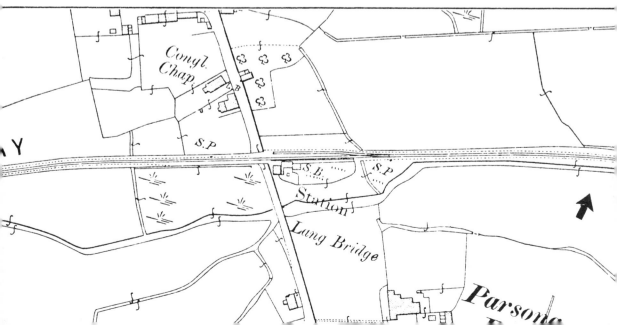

62. No.16 *Ventnor* waits for the cameraman to pick up his case, on 19th July 1955. The station received a direct hit from a bomb in WWII, which may account for the centre of the platform being made of concrete slabs. (P. Hay)

63. The tiny station dealt with a large traffic in flowers to Covent Garden via Sandown and Ryde. This was replaced by tomatoes during WWII, when the Channel Islands were occupied by the enemy. Large quantities of coal and coke were brought into the single siding, which was extended eastwards sometime after this 1908 map was surveyed. (A.W. Burges)

HORRINGFORD

64. Like the previous two stations, the platform was on the south side of the line, but unlike them the single siding was on the same side. From it, there was a spur into a ballast pit. When photographed in 1955, the station was immaculately kept and the single member of staff was always in correct uniform. (P. Hay)

65. The station was little used because it was on the main road between Sandown and Newport which carried a more fequent and cheaper bus service. The charming semi-dormer window has been retained in the metamorphosis to a house and at the same time two full dormers have sprouted out of the roof. (A.W. Burges)

MERSTONE

66. A train of variegated four-wheeled coaches passes the station master's house, on its way from Sandown. The locomotive is IWCR 2–2–2T no.2 *Precursor* and the branch on the right ran to Ventnor Town, as it was then known. The date is circa 1900. (D. Cullum collection)

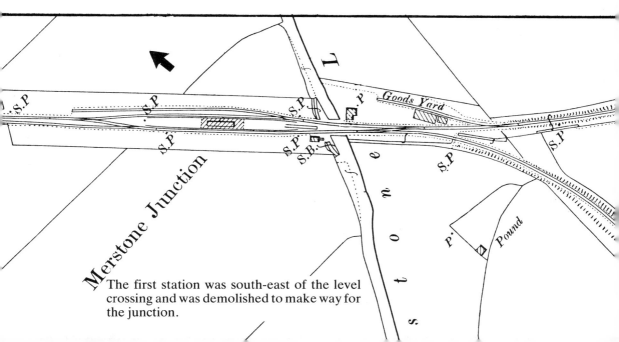

The first station was south-east of the level crossing and was demolished to make way for the junction.

67. Prior to the formation of the SR, access to the island platform was via a subway from either side of the level crossing, as shown on the 1908 map. A pump was provided to fill the locomotive water tank on the left; this was also used to pump out the water which regularly flooded the subway. In the late 1920s, the subway was filled in and a foot crossing provided in its place.
(D. Cullum collection)

68. The Ventnor West branch was commonly operated by a push pull set. Here we see two sets (ex-LCDR) sandwiching Terrier no.13 *Carisbrooke* in 1937 and all standing in the siding at the Newport end of the station.
(S.W. Baker)

69. Looking south-east in 1950, we notice an extra siding by the trees when compared with the 1908 layout. The siding in the previous picture runs from the bottom right of this photograph. Only the trees and the platform remain today. (D. Cullum collection)

DOWN. **WEEK-DAYS.**

Miles.			1	2	3	4	5	6	7	8	9	10	11	12	13	14	15	16
			Goods	Goods	Mxd	Mxd	Pass.	Goods	Pass	Pas	Goods	Pas	Exp.	Pass	Pas	Mxd	Goods	Pass
			a.m	a.m	a.m	a.m	a.m.	a.m.	noon	p.m		p.m	p.m.	p.m	p.m.	p.m	p.m	p.m.
	NEWPORT	dep.	6 30	6 45	7 40	9 5	10 20		12 0	1 5	Newport to Shide 2-0 p.m.	3 10	3 50	5 15	5 20	8 0	8 30	9 10
½	Pan Lane Siding	,,	pass															
1	Shide	dep	pass	7 0	7A44	9A 8	10 A23		Pass	1 A9		3A14	pass	—	5A23	8 A 4	—	9 14
2¼	Blackwater	A		Work Pan and Shide.	7 47	9 12	10 26	B		1 12		3 17	pass	—	5 26	8 8	—	9 18
3¾	MERSTONE Junct.	arr	6 50		7 51	9 16	10 30		12 9	1 17		3 21	4ps0	5 25	5 30	8 12	8 45	9 22
3¾	MERSTONE Junct	dep	To Ventnor		7 53	9 18	10 32	11 15	12 10	1 20		3 23	To Ventnor	To Ventnor	5 32	8 15	9 15	9 24
5¼	Horringford	A			7 57	9 22	10 36	11 20	12 14	1 24		3 27			5 36	8 19	—	9 28
6½	Newchurch	A			8 1	9 26	10 40		12 17	1 27		3 30			5 40	8 22	—	9 31
7¾	Alverstone	A			8 5	9 30	10 44		12 20	1 30		3 34			5 44	8 25	—	9 36
9	SANDOWN	arr.			8 10	9 35	10 48		12 25	1 35		3 38			5 48	8 30	9 45 Saturdays excepted	9 40 Sats. only

A Stops by Signal. **N.B.** Engines must not run coupled between Newport and Merstone Junction.

NOTES. Week-days. B.—Branch Engine work Horringford Pit if necessary.

No. 1 Take all Ventnor Line Wagons. Load sand as required. Shunt Ventnor Yard.

No. 2 Engine of 7-25 Newport to Ryde. Work Pan and Shide to relieve Ventnor Goods.

No. 3. Convey Mew's and Crouchers Sandown Traffic.. No. 7 must run to time. Work through to Ventnor.

ELECTRIC TABLET—Newport, Shide, and M one. **ELECTRIC BLOCK**—Merstone, Newchurch and Sandown.

TELEPHONE.—All Station

UP. **WEEK-DAYS.**

Miles			1	2	3	4	5	6	7	8	9	10	11	12	13	14	15	16	
			Goods	Pass	Mixed	Pass	Goods	Pass	Goods	Mxd	Eng.	Pass.	Pass	Pass	Pass	Gds	Pass	Goods	Goods
			a.m.	a.m.	a.m.	a.m.	a.m.	p.m.		p.m	p.m.	p.m.	p.m.	p.m	p.m.	p.m	p.m	p.m.	p.m.
	SANDOWN	dep.		8 30	9 45	10 55		12 30	Shide to Newport 2-20 p.m.	2 35	From Sandown	3 55	Ex Ventnor	6 0	8 40	Sats. excepted.	9 45	10 0	Saturdays only. Ex Ventnor Branch.
1¼	Alverstone	A		8 34	pass	10 59		12 34		2 39		3 59		6 4	8 44		9 49	Work as required Saturdays excepted	
2½	Newchurch	A		8 37		11 2		12 37		2 42		4 2		6 8	8 47		9 52		
3½	Horringford	A		8 41		11 5	11 35	12 40		2 45		4 6		6 12	8 51		9 55		
5¼	MERSTONE Junct.	arr		8 45	10 3	11 9	11 40	12 45		2 50		4 10		6 17	8 55		10 0		
5¼	MERSTONE Junct	dep		8 47	10 5	11 12		12 47		2 52	3 0	4 12	5 0	6 18	8 58	9 15	10 3	10 30	10 15
6¾	Blackwater	A		8 51	pass	11 16		12 52		2 57	—	4 17	5 4	6 22	9 2		10 8		A
8	Shide	dep	7 10	8A54	pass	11A20		12 A55		3 A1	—	4 21	5 A7	6 A26	9 A 6		10A 12		A
9	NEWPORT	arr	7 15	8 58	10 15	11 24		1 0		3 5	3 10	4 25	5 10	6 30	9 10	9 30	10 15 Sats only.	10 45	10 30

A Stops by Signal.

NOTES Week-days No. 3 Must run to time. Attach Wagons of No. 1 Up Branch at Merstone. No. 5 ex Horringford Pit if necessary. No. 6 must not be held at Sandown after 12-35 p.m. and work to Merstone only.

No. 14 Return of 8-30 p.m. Goods from Newport.

TABLET SECTIONS. Newport, Shide, and Merstone. **STAFF SECTION.** Merstone Junction to Sandown.

October 1909 working timetable.

70. *Godshill* arrives from Newport in September 1952, whilst no.35 *Freshwater*, another O2, stands by the coal stage between trips on the branch. (P. Hay)

71. The 28-lever signal box was the only one on the Island to have wheel operated level crossing gates. (E. Gamblin)

72. We witness the arrival of the 4.08pm
from Sandown on 14th September 1953,
hauled by no.30. The coaches in the goods
yard are not for use on the branch, as that had
closed 12 months earlier. The yard had
despatched up to 19 wagons of sugar beet
daily in previous seasons. (J.H. Aston)

73. This is the approaching passenger's
view, in September 1955. *Yarmouth* was
scrapped in the following year but the brass
star on the smokebox no doubt survived, as it
was the driver's personal embellishment –
nowadays called customising. 14 was the
locomotive duty number. (P. Hay)

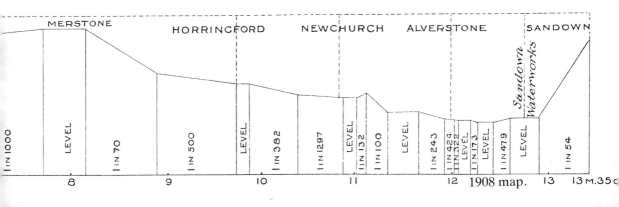

BLACKWATER

Blackwater House

S.P

St. Barnabas' Church

G.P

M.S Newpor

Blackwater Bridge

Station

S.B

G.P

Timber Yd.

Blackwater

Methodist Chapel (Wesleyan)

P.O.

Smithy

S.P

F.B.

74. The house is parallel to the road rather than the railway and survives today, having been extended over the platform and painted white. To the left of the house are the level crossing gates over the main road between Newport and Shanklin. The year is 1921. (Lens of Sutton)

The 1908 map shows the infant River Medina (with dots) being joined by another clear stream from chalk springs, which runs behind the station. After converging, they pass under a road and immediately diverge into two man-made channels *either side* of the railway. This unusual arrangement was presumably to reduce the risk of flooding the line.

75. On 7th September 1953, we witness the arrival of no.36, the highest number used on the old Island railways. Don't miss the large destination board on the train; the extra equipment on the engine for push-pull working; another stretcher cupboard and the discreetly placed door to the Gents. (P. Hay)

SHIDE

Once again the 1908 map shows the intimate relationship of the railway with the River Medina (dotted). Sidings are provided to the goods yard, to the mill and to the chalk quarry. In addition to supplying large quantities of chalk to the Medina Cement Mills, the quarry also produced ballast for the railways from a bed of plateau gravel that overlies the chalk beds in certain areas.

76. The 9-lever signal box behind the station master acted as a block post, which allowed for mineral trains to be easily locked into the sidings. No trace remains of the station today or of the Pan Lane siding to Pan Mill, half way to Newport. (Lens of Sutton)

→

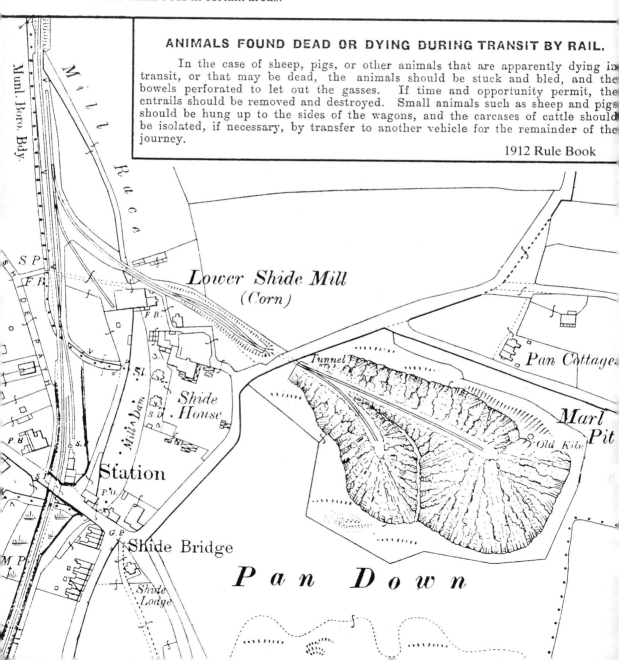

ANIMALS FOUND DEAD OR DYING DURING TRANSIT BY RAIL.

In the case of sheep, pigs, or other animals that are apparently dying in transit, or that may be dead, the animals should be stuck and bled, and the bowels perforated to let out the gasses. If time and opportunity permit, the entrails should be removed and destroyed. Small animals such as sheep and pigs should be hung up to the sides of the wagons, and the carcases of cattle should be isolated, if necessary, by transfer to another vehicle for the remainder of the journey.

1912 Rule Book

77. E on the wagons indicates "Engineers". Ballast continued to be provided from above the quarry long after the chalk traffic ceased in 1944. Unlike the grey granite ballast standard on the mainland, Island railways were ballasted with distinctive brown and white flints. (A.W. Burges)

4. Ventnor West branch

VENTNOR WEST

78. The SR retained the IWCR's number 8 on this 1898 Beyer Peacock, but withdrew the locomotive in November 1929 for scrapping. The covered bunker was an unusual feature. Behind the engine is the station master's house. (D. Cullum collection)

1908

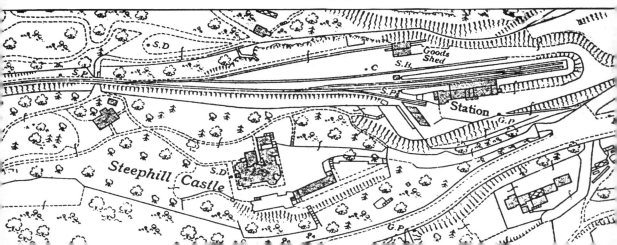

79. No.8 never received a name, although the drivers might have thought of one when her inside motion needed oiling. The water bag is seen entering the cab on 25th June 1928 and a glimpse is obtained of the goods yard crane. (Pamlin Prints)

80. The right hand platform was seldom used, neither indeed was the signal box in latter years. The entire station was extravagant and the concept of the branch over optimistic, although the spiked flat bottom rail was an economy. (Pamlin Prints)

81. This appears to be the same train that we saw at the Merstone coal stage in picture no.70. This time the crew take water alongside the ash pit. Coach no.4112 survives today, in use on the Isle of Wight Steam Railway. (R. Silsbury collection)

82. Ex-LBSCR composite coach no.6987 was regularly used on the branch in 1948-49 as a push-pull unit or motor train, thus rendering the crossover on the left unnecessary. The evening sun illuminates the electric headlights and gossiping crew perfectly. (J.H. Aston)

83. The signal box had 13 levers (2 spare) and could remain unstaffed when working "one engine in steam" on the branch. Merstone box then issued the "long section train staff" to the driver. The board below the station name announced "168 feet above sea level". This was 126ft lower than the former rival terminus. (Lens of Sutton)

84. An unusual visitor to the goods shed on 15th April was coach no.6986, a former LBSCR saloon. It was later converted to the Ryde Works breakdown van. (R. Silsbury collection)

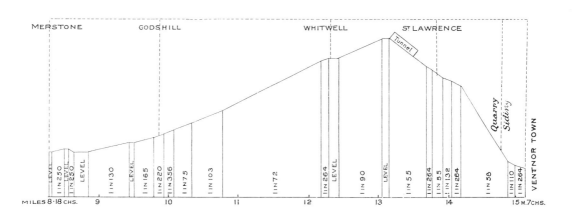

85. In 1952, the branch was visited by a large number of railway enthusiasts, including one who seems to be wearing someone else's trousers. The main purpose of this photo- graph is to show that the signal box interlocking allowed the home *and* starting signals to be pulled off simultaneously. (P. Hay)

BLOCKAGE OF DRAINS.

Drains on the Company's property are sometimes blocked by an accumulation of stiff paper and cotton waste in the pipes. The practice of depositing such materials in the closets must, as far as it can be controlled by the Staff, be discontinued, and the attention of Station Masters and others is drawn to the necessity of seeing that the drains connected with the closets and urinals are thoroughly flushed at least once a day, and proper Sanitary paper supplied for use.

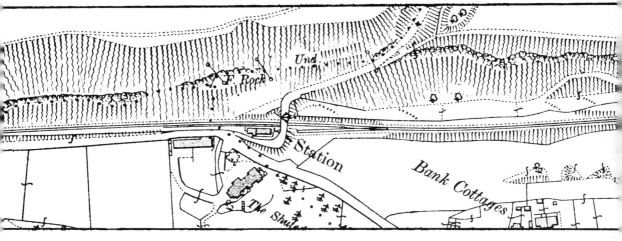

86. The line is on a rising gradient of 1 in 55 at this point. The construction of a station on such a severe incline was not likely to have been approved before the advent of continuous brakes. The station was unstaffed after 1927. (Lens of Sutton)

A short goods siding appears on this 1908 map. A quarry siding existed for some years on the north side of the line, near to Ventnor.

87. The magnificent panorama to be enjoyed on emerging from St. Lawrence tunnel on a clear day was unsurpassed on the Island railways. In the distance is Ventnor Pier, whose future is again in doubt. (S.W. Baker)

88. Freshly painted class O2 *Shorwell* emerges from the south end of the tunnel, on a tight 12-chain curve. Both photographs were taken in July 1937. A treadle in the tunnel operated a warning bell at the foot crossing seen by the train in the previous picture. (S.W. Baker)

WHITWELL

89. A quarter of a mile north of St. Lawrence tunnel the line crossed the B3327. This was the only level crossing on the branch and it surprisingly had the luxury of a footbridge for the rare pedestrian who might be delayed at the gates. (D. Cullum collection)

90. The passing loop is still in position in this view from the signal box, it being taken out of use in 1926 and removed in 1928. All the substantial station buildings on the branch remain standing today, in residential use. (R. Silsbury collection)

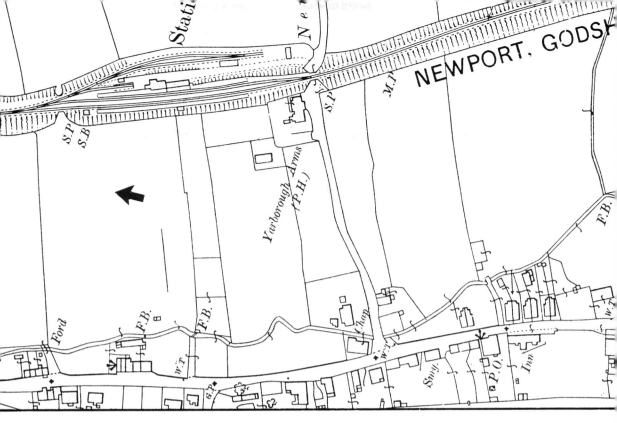

The position of the 10-lever signal box is indicated SB on this 1908 map which not only shows a loop between the platforms but one in the goods yard also.

91. From 1927, train guards acted as conductors to collect the fares, although Whitwell was sometimes staffed in the summer. The prefix W was given by the SR to their Wight engines; no.8 is now one of the two Terriers preserved on the Island. Photo date – 25th July 1935. (S.W. Baker)

GODSHILL

92. This station never brought a large income for the successive railway managers – some agricultural traffic, notably milk, and a few local passengers, until the bus service commenced. The cap appears to be SR style – maybe the managers are visiting their newly acquired station in the mid-1920s. (R.B. Owen collection)

93. The now well known no.8 halts briefly at the grass covered platform on 13th April 1936. The station was surrounded by fields but was only ½ mile from the centre of the village. (S.W. Baker)

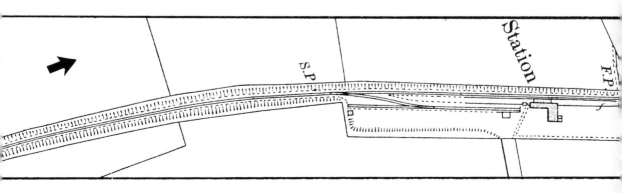

		1	2	3	4	5	6	7	8		9		
		Goods	Mixed	Pass.	Pass.	Pass.	Exprs	Pass	Mixed		Pass		
Miles		a.m.	a.m.	a.m.	noon	p.m.	p.m.	p.m	p.m.		p.m.		
MERSTONE Jct.	dep	7 0	9 18	10 32	12 10	1 20	pass	5 35	8 15		9 24		
1¼ Godshill A	dep	7 15	9 22	10 36	12 13	1 25	4 4	5 39	8 19	Saturdays	9 28		
4 Whitwell	"	7 45	9 29	10 41	12 18	1 31	4 A9	5 45	8 24		9 33		
5¼ St. Lawrence A	"	7 55	9 35	10 45	12 22	1 35	4 A12	5 50	8 31		9 37		
6¾ VENTNOR Town	arr	8 5	9 40	10 50	12 25	1 40	4 15	5 55	8 35		9 40		

A. Stops by Signal.

N.B.   All Passenger Trains must stop momentarily outside Ventnor Home Signals—Goods Trains to stop dead.

NOTES. Week-days.

No. 1 Take all Ventnor Line Wagons Must work to time. Shunt Ventnor Yard on arrival.   Load Sand when required.   No. 3, 4, 6. & 8 Through Trains Cowes to Ventnor Town.

ELECTRIC BLOCK. Merstone Junction, Godshill, Whitwell, Ventnor Town

TELEPHONE.   Same, including St. Lawrence.

		1	2	3	4	5	6	7	8		9		
		Mixed	Pass	Pass.	Pass.	Mixed	Pass.	Pass.	Pass		Pass		
Miles		a.m.	a.m.	a.m.	noon	p.m.	p.m.	p.m.	p.m.		p.m.		
VENTNOR Town	dep	8 25	9 45	10 55	12 30	2 35	4 45	6 0	8 40		9 45		
1¼ St. Lawrence A		8 30	9 50	10 59	12 34	2 39	4 49	6 4	8 44	Sats. only	9 49		
2¾ Whitwell	dep.	8 35	9 55	11 3	12 38	2 43	4 53	6 8	8 48		9 53		
5¼ Godshill A		8 40	9 59	11 7	12 42	2 47	4 57	6 12	8 52		9 57		
6¾ MERSTONE Jct.	arr.	8 45	10 2	11 10	12 46	2 50	4 59	6 15	8 55		10 0		

NOTES.—Week-days.   A Calls by Signal.

No. 1 to bring all Ventnor Line Wagons   Heavy Engine.   Must run to time.

No. 3 4. & 6 Must run to time. Through Trains to Cowes.

STAFF SECTION. Merstone Junction to Whitwell. Whitwell to Ventnor Town.

1909 working timetable.

5. Freshwater – Newport

FRESHWATER

94. This Edwardian postcard reveals the type of transport on offer to travellers wishing to extend their journey to Totand Bay or Alum Bay to view The Needles. On the left is the parapet wall of Bow Bridge which crossed one of the headwaters of the River Yar. (D. Cullum collection)

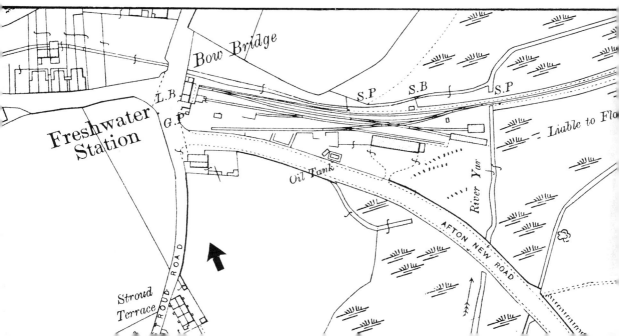

95. In 1906 the IWCR introduced its new steam railcar onto the branch. The crew are in the shadow, making adjustments to the engine unit, details of which are given with picture 19 in *Ryde to Ventnor*. All steam railcars suffered the disadvantage of restricted capacity at peak times whereas a locomotive could haul an extra coach or two. (National Railway Museum)

96. After its divorce from the IWCR in 1913, the FYNR acquired its own rolling stock which included this charming Drewry railcar. It sat 12 (15 at a pinch) and was often used for conveyance of passengers from a late running Lymington ferry. It seems that the back rests were reversible (as on a tramcar) and that the vehicle was in use for about 10 years. A replica could make useful income in off-peak time at Haven Street nowadays. (R. Silsbury collection)

NEWPORT, YARMOUTH, and FRESHWATER.—Southern (late Freshwater, Yarmouth, and Newport).

1924.

Down.			Week Days.							Sundays.				
	mrn	mrn	mrn	aft	aft	aft	aft	aft	aft	mrn	aft	aft	aft	aft
									S					
Newport...............dep	8 57	1027	1152	1 23	3 23	4 52	6 22	6 56	7 56	9 27	1027	1231	2 15	4 10	7 16
1½ Carisbrooke Halt. for Castle	9 3	1033	1153	1 28	3 28	4 58	6 28	7 2	8 2	9 33	1061	1231	2 21	4 16	7 19
5½ Calbourne, fr Shalfleet & Bright	9 14	1044	12 9	1 3½3	3 9½5	9 6	3 9½7	13 8	13 9	44	1042	1242	2 33	4 27	7 27
7 Ningwood...........[stone	9 16	1045	1213	1 43	3 45	13 6	4 27	19 5	16 9	48	1056	1242	2 56	4 31	7 31
10 Yarmouth 159	9 26	1056	1221	1 51	3 51	5 15	2 16	5 17	27 8	27 9	56	1054	1251	2 41	4 39	7 39
12 Freshwater † ....arr	9 31	11 1	1226	1 56	3 56	5 56	2 66	5 67	32 8	32 10	1	1059	1259	2 47	4 47	7 44

Up.			Week Days.							Sundays.				
	mrn		mrn	mrn	aft	aft	aft	aft	aft	aft	mrn	aft	aft	aft	aft
Freshwater.............dep	8 5		8 45	11 5	1238	2 8	4 8	5 38	7 53	5		11 01	58	554	50 9	0
2 Yarmouth	8 10		8 50	1113	1243	2 18	4 18	5 43	7 10	8 10		11 31	108	04	558	5
5 Ningwood...........[Brightstone	8 18		8 59	1121	1251	2 21	4 21	5 51	7 18	8 18		11 31	143	85	36	13
6½ Calbourne, for Shalfleet and	8 23		10 2	1125	1258	2 28	4 28	5 58	7 28	8 23		11 27	143	125	7 8	17
10½ Carisbrooke Halt. for Castle	8 34		1013	1153	1 6	2 36	4 56	5 6	7 7	38 8	34	1155	163	235	158	23
12 Newport 154, 150 ....arr	8 41		1020	1143	1 13	2 43	4 56	1 47	47 8	41		1145	403	305	258	35

S Saturdays only.

† Station for Totland Bay (1½ miles), Alum Bay (2¾ miles), and The Needles (3½ miles).

97. Tank wagons were few in number on the Island and presumably carried paraffin for domestic heating and cooking. An oil tank is shown on the map. The Southern Railway scrapped all the light flat-bottom rail seen here. (National Railway Museum)

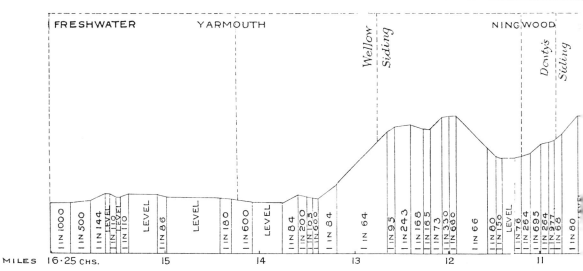

	Week Days.					**Sundays.**					**Week Days**						**Sundays.**		
	gov 1&2	1&2	1&2			1&2	1&2	1&2			gov 1&2	1&2	1&2	1&2				1&2	1&2
	mrn	aft	aft	aft		aft	aft	mrn	aft	aft		mrn	mrn	aft	aft	aft	aft		aft	mrn aft
Freshwater	9 42	1229	2 18	4 25		5 45	7 6	8 4	5	7 39	Newport dp	9 2	1125	1 53	5 5	15	6 23		8 53	9 38 4 40
Yarmouth	9 47	1225	2 23	4 30		5 50	7 6	8 50	3 50	7 44	Carisbrooke	9 7	1131	1 11	3 11		6 29		9 1	1144 4 46
Ningwood	9 55	1234	2 32	4 39		5 58	Sig.	9 8	3 58	7 52	Calborne*	9 19	1143	1 23	3 23		Sig.		9 1	1154 4 57
Calborne*	10 0	1239	2 37	4 44		6 3	Sig.	9 2	4	7 57	Ningwood	9 23	1148	1 29	3 29		Sig.		9 1	1158 7 3
Carisbrooke	1010	1251	2 49	4 56			7 28	9 18	4 18	8 7	Yarmouth	9 31	1157	1 38	3 38	3 38	6 49		9 24	12 6 7 11
Newport	89	1017	125	2 56	5 3		6 19	7 31	9 19	4 18	8 13	Frshwater†	9 37	12 3	1 43	3 43	3 43	5 40	6 57		9 34	1218 7 15

* Calborne and Shalfleet. † Station for Totland Bay, Alum Bay, and the Needles.

1890

98. *Bembridge* having cleared the points, the driver looks at the signalman to wait for a nod, on 10th September 1953. The signal box subsequently served as a bus shelter nearby before returning to its proper function at Wootton. (R.C. Riley)

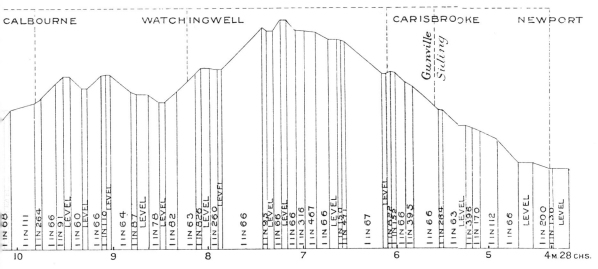

99. A minute or so later no.33 pulls away to run round its train, revealing a discrepancy in platform heights. The platform was extended at least four times; in 1932 and 1936 it was due to the increasing length of *The Tourist* from Ventnor. (R.C. Riley)

100. The signal box had been at the FYNR station at Newport until 1927. When it was moved here, it was placed close to the station so that it could be worked by the station staff. (R.B. Owen)

ISLE OF WIGHT & NEWPORT JUNCTION RAILWAYS.

RAIL AND COACH EXCURSIONS.

Freshwater, for Alum Bay and the Needles!!

BY COACH FROM VENTNOR.

On and after Saturday, April 20th, a Four-Horse Coach, "The Rocket," will leave the Bonchurch Hotel at 9.40 a.m., Ventnor Station at 10.5 a.m. daily (Sundays excepted), passing Sandrock, Blackgang, Chale, Shorwell, Brixton and Brooke.

This Excursion affords unrivalled advantages for viewing the magnificent Scenery of the Undercliff, and the Picturesque Villages of the Southern Coast of the Island.

THROUGH TICKETS ISSUED FROM STATIONS AS UNDER:—

Via VENTNOR COACH. FROM	By Train leaving at	FARES THERE & BACK.	
		1st Class.	2nd Class.
	a. m.	s. d.	s. d.
Ryde (St. John's)	9 25	12 3	11 9
Brading	9 33	11 3	10 9
Newport (Pan Lane) ..	9 5	12 6	11 6
Shide	9 8	12 6	11 6
Horringford	9 22	11 3	10 6
Sandown	9 39	10 6	10 3
Shanklin	9 46	10 3	10 0
Wroxall	9 55	9 3	9 0

The Coach returns in time to save the 7.40 p.m. Train for Ryde and Newport.

☞ **Notice as to issue of Rail and Coach Tickets.**—These Tickets are available for return on the day of issue only, and are issued for the convenience of Passengers, but the Company give notice they will not be responsible for the Coach Conveyance ; also that they cannot guarantee any particular seat by the Coach, either inside or outside. The class refers to the Railway portion of the journey only.

Children occupying seats will be charged full price.

Isle of Wight & Newport Junction Railways.

COMMENCEMENT OF THE

COACHING SEASON

On and after SATURDAY, April 20th,
BETWEEN

Newport (Pan Mill Station) & Freshwater,
FOR

YARMOUTH, ALUM BAY AND THE NEEDLES!

Forming direct Communication with Trains from Ryde, Sandown, Shanklin, Ventnor and intermediate Stations.

Daily (Sundays excepted), a well-appointed Four-Horse Coach, "The Express," will leave the Newport Station of the Newport Junction Railway on the arrival of the 11.28 a.m. Train from Ryde and Ventnor.

THROUGH TICKETS ISSUED FROM STATIONS AS UNDER:

Via NEWPORT COACH. FROM	By Train leaving at	FARES THERE & BACK.	
		1st Class.	2nd Class.
	A.M.	s. d.	s. d.
Ryde (St. John's)	10 55	7 6	6 9
Brading	11 4	7 9	7 3
Ventnor	10 35	9 0	8 0
Wroxall	10 41	8 6	7 9
Shanklin	10 49	7 9	7 3
Sandown	11 10	7 6	7 0
Horringford ..	11 15	6 3	6 0

The Coach returns in time to save the 6.15 p.m. Train for Ryde and Ventnor.

☞ **Notice as to issue of Rail and Coach Tickets.**—These Tickets are available for Return on day of issue only, and are issued for the convenience of Passengers, but the Company give notice they will not be responsible for the Coach Conveyance ; also that they cannot guarantee any particular seat by the Coach, either inside or outside. The class refers to the Railway portion of the journey only. Children occupying seats will be charged full price.

ISLE OF WIGHT & NEWPORT JUNCTION RAILWAYS.

RAIL AND COACH EXCURSIONS
TO

FRESHWATER,

FOR YARMOUTH, ALUM BAY AND THE NEEDLES,
DIRECT FROM

Ventnor and Newport (Pan Mill) Railway Stations
DURING THE

TOURIST SEASON.

Commencing SATURDAY, April 20th.

Arrangements have been made for the issue of

CIRCULAR TICKETS

From all Stations in connection with the above, enabling Passengers to proceed by Train to Ventnor, thence by Coach to Freshwater, passing Blackgang Chine, Chale, Shorwell, Brixton and Brooke, and returning by Coach to Newport, passing Carisbrooke Castle, thence by the Newport Junction Railway, or

Passengers may go viâ Newport and return viâ Ventnor.

Fares for the whole Round. FROM	1st Class.	2nd Class.
	s. d.	s. d.
RYDE (St. John's)	12 '6	11 3
BRADING	12 0	11 0
SANDOWN		
SHANKLIN		
WROXALL	11 0	10 6
VENTNOR		
HORRINGFORD		
SHIDE		
NEWPORT		

☞ These Circular Tickets will be available for return within One Week. For Coach times and Trains in connection, see previous announcements, pages 6 and 7.

Notice as to issue of Rail and Coach Tickets.—These Tickets are issued for the convenience of Passengers, but the Company give notice they will not be responsible for the Coach conveyance ; also that they cannot guarantee any particular seat by the Coach, either inside or outside. The class refers to the Railway portion of the journey only. Children occupying seats will be charged full price.

EXCURSIONS
FROM

ISLE OF WIGHT
AND

Newport Junction Railway Stations,

To BLACKGANG, viâ VENTNOR and

JACKMAN'S CHARS-A-BANC.

Daily, Sundays excepted, as under:—

				FARES.			
				1st Sngl.	1st Rtn.	2nd Sngl.	2nd Rtn.
	a.m.	a.m.	a.m.	s. d.	s. d.	s. d.	s. d.
Leaving Ryde(St. Jn's. Rd.)at	9 25	10 55	2 15	5 0	7 3	4 0	6 9
Brading ..	9 33	11 4	2 23	4 0	6 0	3 4	5 5
Sandown ..	9 39	11 9	2 29	3 6	5 4	3 2	5 1
Newport Pan Lane	9 5	10 35	..	5 0	7 0	4 5	6 0
Shide ..	9 8	10 38	..	5 0	7 0	4 5	6 0
Horringford ..	9 22	10 43	..	4 1	5 9	3 8	5 0
Shanklin ..	9 46	11 15	2 36	3 3	5 0	2 10	4 8
Wroxall ..	9 55	11 23	2 45	2 6	3 10	2 4	3 7

Returning in time for the 2.10 p.m., 5.25 p.m., and 6.25 p.m. Trains from Ventnor.

These Tickets are available for Return on the day of issue only, and are issued for the convenience of Passengers, but the Company give notice they will not be responsible for, nor will they guarantee any particular seat by the Road Conveyance. The Class refers to the Railway portion of the journey only.

CHILDREN UNDER TWELVE HALF-PRICE.

YARMOUTH

101. Because of the proximity of the tidal mill pond, the down platform was not opposite the up. This view was taken from the down platform and just shows the corner of the signal box on the right. (Lens of Sutton)

The two northern sidings on this 1897 map did not appear on the 1908 edition.

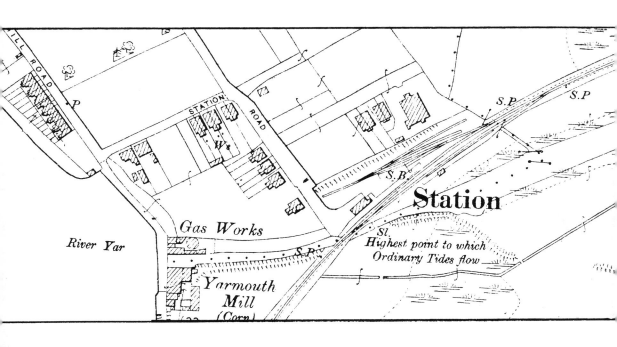

102. In 1937, the down platform was still evident. Terrier no.11 *Newport* (now at Haven Street) rattles over the goods yard points on 17th September of that year. (S.W. Baker)

103. Eleven days before closure, *Alverstone* heads off towards Freshwater and passes across the bridge over the River Yar. The building is now used as a youth club. (R.C. Riley)

NINGWOOD

104. The station master's house is visible beyond the up platform shelter and appears on the 1908 map. The double arch bridge has only recently been demolished.
(R. Silsbury collection)

105. An enthusiasts' special on 18th May 1952 produced a well groomed *Bonchurch* and a crop of baggy trousers. The passing loop was lengthened in 1936 to 400ft., to accommodate *The Tourist*. (L. Elsey)

Wellow siding served a brickworks in Lee Copse, halfway between Yarmouth and Ningwood.

106. A rare photograph of Ningwood showing a waiting passenger. The water tank was also erected in the 1930s. The 9-lever signal box seen on the down platform acted as a block post and could be closed during slack times, a long section token then being used for the whole branch. (J.H. Aston)

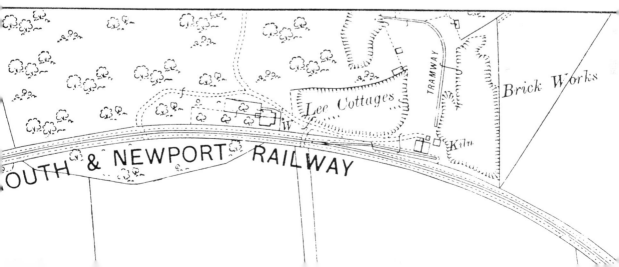

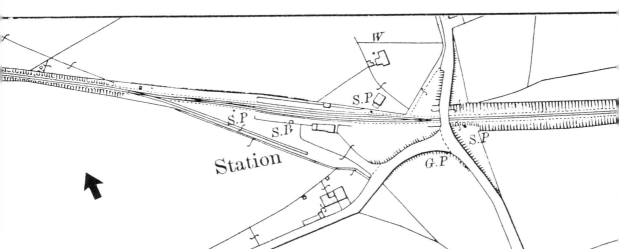

Station

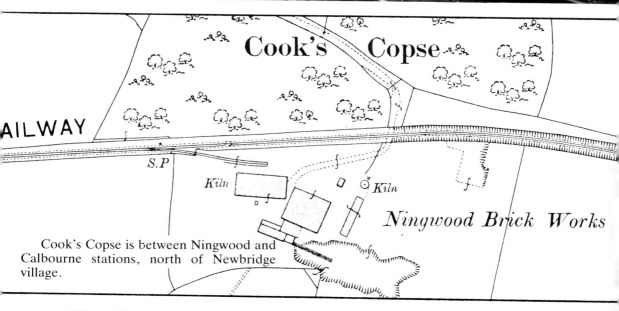

Cook's Copse is between Ningwood and Calbourne stations, north of Newbridge village.

1909 working timetable.

		DOWN.			WEEK-DAYS.						
		1	2	3	4	5	6	7	8		
		Mail & Goods	Pass.	Mixed	Pass	Pass	Mixed	Pass	Pass		
Miles		a.m.	a.m.	a.m.	p.m.	p.m.	p.m.	p.m.	p.m.	Saturdays only.	
	NEWPORT dep	4 30	9 2	11 30	1 10	3 15	4 35	6 40	9 15		
1¼	Carisbrooke dep	—	9 9	11A37	1 17	3 A22	4 48	6 47	9A22		
3¾	Watchingwell A	—	9 14	11 42	1 22	...	4 53	6 52	9 28		
5¼	Calbourne dep	4 50	9 19	11 A47	1A27	3A32	4 58	6A56	9 32		
6¼	Ningwood dep	5 5	9 23	11A52	1A32	3A37	5 4	7A 1	9 37		
9¼	Yarmouth dep	5 30	9 32	12 0	1 40	3 45	5 10	7 10	9 45		
12	FRESHWATER arr	5 40	9 37	12 5	1 45	3 50	5 15	7 15	9 50		

A Calls by signal.

NOTES.—Weekdays. No. 1 Take forward all Goods traffic. Unload Mails and shunt at Yarmouth as required. Must reach Freshwater by 5-45 a.m. Shunt at Freshwater and return with 8-15 a.m. train. No. 2 must work to time. No. 3. To convey none but urgent Wagons. No. 5 must work to time. Stop at Watchingwell for Tenants only. No. 6 Cross No. 5 Up at Carisbrooke. Train to be left at Freshwater for 8-15 a.m. working

CALBOURNE

←

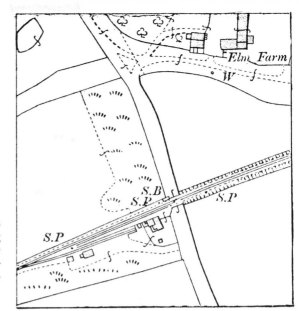

107. The single siding was controlled by a ground frame and the booking office housed the block instrument. The main building of this charming country station has unfortunately now been altered beyond recognition. (R. Silsbury collection)

108. The corrugated iron building on this side of the station was the former booking office at the Newport FYNR terminus. *Chale* is seen leaving eastwards on 7th September 1953, passing one of the many signals built by the SR from a pair of old rails. (P. Hay)

UP.			1	2	3	4	5		6		7	8		9		WEEK-DAYS.
			Mixed	Pass	Mixed	Pass	Mxd.		Goods		Pass	Pass		Mixed		
Miles			a.m.	a.m.	noon	p.m.	p.m.		p.m		p.m.	p.m.		p.m.		
	FRESHWATER	dep	8 15	9 42	12 20	2 25	4 20	Sats. excepted	5 45	Saturdays only	6 0	7 20	Saturdays only	10 0		
2½	Yarmouth	dep	8 20	9 47	12 25	2 30	4 25		5 50		6 5	7 25		10 5		
5	Ningwood	dep	8A30	9 55	12 33	2 38	4 33		6 5		6 13	7A 33		10A 14		
6½	Calbourne	dep	8A35	10 0	12 38	2A43	4 38		6 13		6 17	7A 38		10A 18		
8½	Watchingwell	A	8 42	10 4	12 42	2 47	4 42		6 20		6 21	7 42		10A 22		
10¾	Carisbrooke	dep	8 50	10 10	12 48	2A53	4 48		6 28		6A 27	7A 49		10A 28		
12	NEWPORT	arr	8 55	10 17	12 55	3 0	4 55		6 35		6 35	7 55		10 35		

A Calls by signal.

NOTES. Weekdays

No. 2 must run to time.

No. 6 Goods Train except Saturdays.   Cross No. 7 Down at Carisbrooke when work requires.

WATCHINGWELL

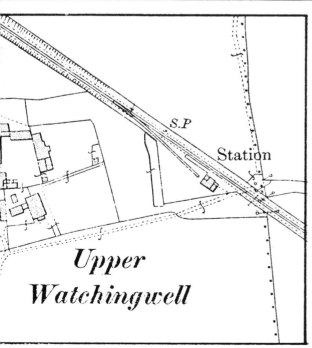

109. This was originally a private station for the use of Sir John Stephen Barrington Simion of Swainstone House but became a public request stop. A double arm signal stood on the platform which was set to indicate whether the train was required to stop or not. The SR replaced it by two distant signals. The station mistress' kitchen doubled up as a booking office. This remote outpost was recorded on film as the closure notice had begun to peel.
(R. Silsbury collection)

110. Until the coming of the buses, this was a fairly important station with two platforms and a passing loop. The SR reduced it to a single platform halt in 1927. The photograph must be from early this century, as no.8 was built in 1898 and the IWCR ceased to work the branch in 1913.
(National Railway Museum)

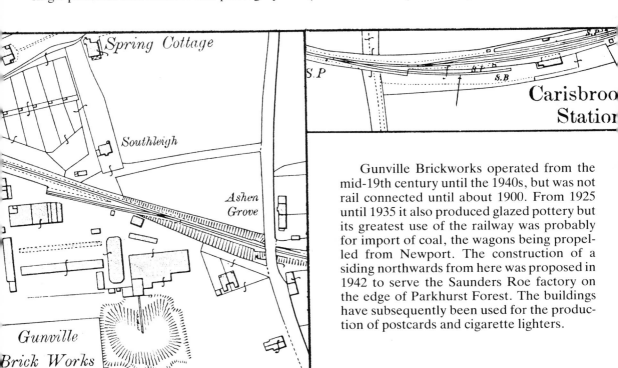

Gunville Brickworks operated from the mid-19th century until the 1940s, but was not rail connected until about 1900. From 1925 until 1935 it also produced glazed pottery but its greatest use of the railway was probably for import of coal, the wagons being propelled from Newport. The construction of a siding northwards from here was proposed in 1942 to serve the Saunders Roe factory on the edge of Parkhurst Forest. The buildings have subsequently been used for the production of postcards and cigarette lighters.

111. Looking towards Newport on 29th March 1949, we see the locomotive passing over the points to the siding, the buffer stops of which stand out clearly in white. New sleepers remind us that little repair work was done during WWII to the track, other than to bomb damage, notably near Whippingham, between Newchurch and Alverstone and on the Cowes line. (R.C.J. Day)

112. Two weeks before closure, *Freshwater* leaves the grass platform on its way to Newport, with Gunville Brickworks just showing in the distance. (P. Hay)

113. No.31 *Chale* has reached the northern outskirts of Newport on 25th July 1935 and is running onto the beginning of a 19-span trestle structure which linked with a series of brick clad arches. (S.W. Baker)

114. Two years later we see the same locomotive (having been turned round in the interim) traversing the first of the nine arches of Towngate or Hunny Hill Viaduct, which carried the line over the main road to Cowes. (S.W. Baker)

NEWPORT

115. With the end of the viaduct in the background, the Drewry railcar waits at the combined up home and down starting signals on 12th May 1919. The home-made cattle wagon is standing on one of the two sidings in the independent goods yard, which also contained an engine shed, partly obscured by the railcar. (K. Nunn/LCGB)

116. In the foreground is the timber platform hurriedly erected in 1913 by the FYNR, carrying several wooden seats and a massive weighing machine. In the background are the workshops of the unfriendly IWCR and some wagons loaded with sawn timber, a commodity not often seen in Island railway photographs. (D. Cullum collection)

117. FYNR locomotive no.2 retained the same number in SR ownership but it was changed to W8 in 1932. Here we can examine some of the ex-Manchester, Sheffield and Lincolnshire Railway coaches acquired from the Great Central Railway by the disgruntled directors in 1913. The platform has both oil and electric lighting. (R. Silsbury collection)

(Railway Magazine)

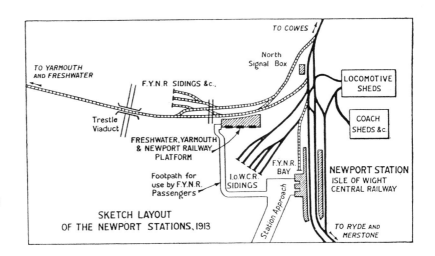

SKETCH LAYOUT
OF THE NEWPORT STATIONS, 1913

118. The other engine acquired by the FYNR in 1913 was this Manning Wardle saddle tank. It was their no.1 and became SR no.W1 but was never renumbered as it was scrapped in 1932. Built in 1902, it was the youngest engine to run on the Island in the pre-preservation era. (J.G. Sturt)

120. Much photographed no.W8 *Freshwater* stands in the Freshwater bay with the North signal box in the distance. Departing trains for the branch had to reverse as far as this box, collect the token and then proceed round the 9-11 chain curve onto the viaduct. (R. Silsbury collection)

119. Terrier no.10 *Cowes* was on the Island from 1900 until 1936 and is seen here hauling a train of ageing ex-LCDR four wheelers past the site of the earlier FYNR terminus, en route for Freshwater on 22nd July 1935. The leading luggage van was formerly a hearse on the LCDR. (S.W. Baker)

121. *Shorwell* grinds round the same sharp curve on 18th May 1952 with the 12.18pm departure for Freshwater. The home signal post is ex-LSWR, reused during the SR modernisation. (P. Hay)

123. The train had only two weeks left to run when these two photographs were taken in September 1953. The luggage doors seem sound but the guard's door has been patched with steel, as has the end panel where the ducket used to be located. The destination board epitomises the golden age of Island steam, when one could rest one's head on a first-class antimacassar for 1 hour 20 minutes and watch the shadows of the exhaust from the engine race across the rolling meadows of "England's Garden Isle". (P. Hay)

122. To many of the thousands of holiday-makers staying in the resorts of south-east Wight, the highlight of the holiday was a trip on *The Tourist* to the western extremity of the Island. This was one of the few fast trains (apart from *The Invalid Express* referred to in *Ryde to Ventnor*) and for many summers departed from Ventnor at 10am, returning from Freshwater at 5.20pm. This coach had a central toilet compartment when in use on the SECR but seats for fare paying passengers were thought to be more appropriate to Island use. (P. Hay)

MP Middleton Press

BRANCH LINES
Vic Mitchell and Keith Smith

BRANCH LINES TO MIDHURST	0 906520 01 0
BRANCH LINES TO HORSHAM	0 906520 02 9
BRANCH LINE TO SELSEY	0 906520 04 5
BRANCH LINES TO EAST GRINSTEAD	0 906520 07 X
BRANCH LINES TO ALTON	0 906520 11 8
BRANCH LINE TO HAYLING	0 906520 12 6
BRANCH LINE TO SOUTHWOLD	0 906520 15 0
BRANCH LINE TO TENTERDEN	0 906520 21 5
BRANCH LINES TO NEWPORT	0 906520 26 6

SOUTH COAST RAILWAYS
Vic Mitchell and Keith Smith

BRIGHTON TO WORTHING	0 906520 03 7
WORTHING TO CHICHESTER	0 906520 06 1
CHICHESTER TO PORTSMOUTH	0 906520 14 2
BRIGHTON TO EASTBOURNE	0 906520 16 9
RYDE TO VENTNOR	0 906520 19 3

SOUTHERN MAIN LINES
Vic Mitchell and Keith Smith

WOKING TO PORTSMOUTH	0 906520 25 8

STEAMING THROUGH
Peter Hay

STEAMING THROUGH KENT	0 906520 13 4
STEAMING THROUGH EAST HANTS	0 906520 18 5
STEAMING THROUGH EAST SUSSEX	0 906520 22 3

OTHER RAILWAY BOOKS

INDUSTRIAL RAILWAYS OF THE SOUTH-EAST	0 906520 09 6
WAR ON THE LINE The official history of the SR in World War II	0 906520 10 X
GARRAWAY FATHER AND SON The story of two unique railway careers.	0 906520 20 7

OTHER SUSSEX BOOKS

MIDHURST TOWN – THEN & NOW	0 906520 05 3
EAST GRINSTEAD – THEN & NOW	0 906520 17 7
THE GREEN ROOF OF SUSSEX A refreshing amble along the South Downs Way.	0 906520 08 8
THE MILITARY DEFENCE OF WEST SUSSEX	0 906520 23 1
WEST SUSSEX WATERWAYS	0 906520 24 X